THE SURFBOARD

By the Same Author

Crap Towns (co-edited by Sam Jordison)
I Fought the Law
The Book of Idle Pleasures (with Tom Hodgkinson)
Three Men in a Float (with Ian Vince)
Planes, Trains and Automobiles
The Idle Traveller

THE SURFBOARD

How using my hands
helped unlock my mind

DAN KIERAN

unbound

This edition first published in 2018

Unbound
6th Floor Mutual House, 70 Conduit Street,
London W1S 2GF

www.unbound.com

Limited edition cover image © yoshi0511/Shutterstock.com

Text Design by Patty Rennie

A CIP record for this book is available
from the British Library

ISBN 978-1-78352-638-3 (trade hbk)
ISBN 978-1-78352-640-6 (ebook)
ISBN 978-1-78352-639-0 (limited edition)

Printed and bound in Great Britain
by Clays Ltd, Elcograf S.p.A.

For Isobel, Wilf, Olive and Ted

PROLOGUE

The evening kindled at the end of a long, speechless day. I had settled into myself as the miles fell on leaving London. Seven hours to ponder the week ahead. The car was now connected to me. We urged each other along. Humming together.

James lived in Cornwall on the north coast by the sea. I had a map drawn from memory after a gin-soaked evening of garrulous optimism in the depths of Wales. 'I live there because the first time I saw the landscape it spoke to me. It's real. That idea you spoke about. It's real.'

We'd met at the Do Lectures on the edge of Cardigan Bay. A weekend of talks and workshops attended by people at an inflection point in their lives. I was invited to give a talk about an idea that had 'had' me. It led indirectly to the founding of the business I now run. When I finished speaking, he and I queued for dinner and then sat next to each other to eat. We hit it off the way you do with strangers only rarely. He told me about his workshop on the remote, battered north coast of Cornwall and I pictured him as a Western version of a guru from the East. A wise man from my own land. One who drew on the same well of home as me.

It was almost a year later to the day. The middle of June. Rain came down so heavily the windscreen wipers made little difference as I skirted the New Forest, turning the A27 into a river as I squinted my way, the flickering brake lights kaleidoscoped by the water battering my windscreen. The torrent soon became too thick to see the woodland from a thousand years before William the Conqueror had declared his hunting domain. The line of cars became a spent dribble as I headed west. The rain helped somehow. The car felt safe. Cosy.

I saw the sign for West Compton, waved to a friend I didn't have time to stop and see, and then passed Long Bredy, where the land would unfurl away from sight towards the sea. I'd stopped in Long and Little Bredy many years before without realising the church we'd parked outside was full of graves marked with the names of my distant family. I had sensed a connection to that place then. I could make out the landscape murmuring to me. I juddered up a steep, short hill. Shifted down a gear and drifted over the top.

It was the day after my forty-first birthday. I was coming to terms with who I had become, which was not someone I ever expected to be. For the first time in a long time I was looking back. The previous decade had been a process of continuous change. After the financial crash of 2008 I lost my livelihood overnight as a writer and, with no qualifications or university degree, had to go back to working daily contracts for minimum wage. On my lunch hour, while clearing out the rat-infested basement of an accountants' firm in Bognor Regis, I had an idea for what had, over the next eight years, grown into a multimillion-pound, global publishing company. But my marriage had collapsed in the process, taking me away from my two beloved children, and I was now engaged, with another baby on the way. I caught my eye in the car's rear-view mirror. How had a description like that ever come to describe me?

PROLOGUE

I realised as I sped along how much I needed some time away. I was struggling to deliver on all the things required of me. To be a good father, fiancé, friend, CEO, employer and employee. Even ex-husband if that was possible. I wasn't sure the ability to be all these things was within me. There had been times of pressure in my life before but they had always come and gone. Now, pausing to reflect, it felt as though it had never stopped.

Staring as the treadmill of tarmac peeled away, I began thinking about the things I could have done and who I could have been. Like any attempt to live an honest life, mine had been messy, but in my bones I knew I was living the right one. I didn't believe the sadness or blind turns I'd experienced meant I'd gone wrong. Each episode was just the path I'd taken to gain a different perspective on who I would become.

I was in a dark place, though. Gravitating towards the kinds of books people read when trying to work out what gives life meaning. I read them slightly desperately, devouring them among harassed commuters, but soon realised all espoused the same, slightly unrealistic philosophy.

You had to remove yourself from the distractions of normal life completely. You had to go on a journey inside your own mind. Through meditation. Or fasting. Shunning work. But I had significant responsibilities I couldn't just up and leave. Reading these books after starting a family and having signed up to long-term financial obligations became just another cause of anxiety. I worried whether the fact I was mid-life, surrounded by people I loved and with a decent job, meant self-knowledge, a life of meaning, was beyond me. And work weighed heavily. I was about to embark on a phase of stress I knew would stretch me more than I wanted it to. I thought it might break me.

Cornwall arrived hours later on a sign as I swept past Exeter, but the north coast I was heading for was still far away. Darkness in June takes a while to settle, as though the night can't quite make up its mind to come. A few pondering hours later the road climbed, became my horizon and turned into cloud before falling as the unseen land funnelled towards the sea. The beach I arrived at was desolate. A few lonely gulls drifting across the vast expanse of sand. Grey houses people yearn to escape from clutched to the cliffs next to empty cottages with glass extensions borrowed by strangers searching for summer sun. I opened the car door, pushing it with my right foot against the wind. The surf pounded. It fizzed.

I looked at the drawing which I had transferred from his description of the landscape that had spoken to him into my notebook so many months ago, and fought east up a hill on foot until I convinced myself the picture – albeit from a different angle – matched the scene beneath me. I was out of breath and bent my body over, pushing my hands down on my knees to draw in air and recover, and felt pleased I had made it. It was the right place. I stood up and stretched my back, pushing my shoulders behind my body. At the top of the hill to my right I could see a crack of a path leading through what I imagined was green, turning into a slow-declining road that fell gently north to my left to the sea. James's house was in the distance somewhere and this was the view he lived to see. The view that had connected him through the idea to me. There was a car park at the bottom of the road with a small hut and a payment machine. I looked at it from the west. The declivity of the road and the cliffs ahead hid the endless sea. If you dared to venture far enough through the gap, it would seem as though the beach of the world had been hiding behind it. Waves curled through the apparently flat water below like fabric with an evolving seam. A mix of geography, power and dream. Something even a non-surfer like me could see.

An hour later I had found my campsite and unpacked myself into a canvas bell tent with a double bed and duvet, a table to eat on and a rug next to a chest of pans, glasses, mugs and candles because there was no electricity. I'd left my phone at home as a statement of intent. I wrote thoughts in my notebook until the light dwindled behind a quilt of cloud and then read the flames while imagining the sea. My kettle steamed on the brazier and soon I was warming inside from drenched mint leaves. I planned to have no alcohol that week and plenty of sleep. There was a phone booth by the road in case of emergencies and a postbox if my notebook got the better of me. I wrote down the phone number on a postcard in my back pocket to send to my love the next morning so she could reach me. I turned to the mattress and candles in the tent.

If you are on a journey to find out who you are, you'll find clues reflected in the people you meet. My mind had evolved so slowly I was unaware of the changes but I knew it was happening tectonically. Looking back, my life had experienced dramatic shifts, both professionally and personally, but at the time it didn't seem so. Not especially. I had spent most of my life following something instead of leading. Despite now being beyond forty, I still felt essentially the same as at fifteen. The only exception being a strange kind of gaunt experience garnered from living through love, loss and tragedy.

I was adjusting to middle age. From the outside my life choices had always appeared erratic. Maybe even mercurial. Especially a few years before, but they made elemental sense to me. The reflection I cast in the people around me, I'd decided, was my most effective 'real-time' way of glimpsing me. Meeting him was the first time I hadn't discovered one of these mirrors retrospectively.

But I had hit a wall inside my own mind. Reaching the edge of what I thought I was capable of being. In my life. The business. Everything. It was an emergency. I had to prove to myself somehow that the preconceptions I had accepted my entire life did not have to be defining.

There is one limitation I have held as being unquestionably true for as long as I can remember. It had become one of the indelible truths of my personality. An art teacher once told me I was not 'the kind of person' who can make things with their hands. And she was right. I am incapable of making anything. I don't own tools. A few days before leaving for Cornwall I had broken a barbecue while trying to build it. I'm hopeless with my hands. Always have been. I'm too impatient to try to understand instruction booklets. So coming down here was a throw of the dice. The impact of failure would be calcifying. But if I could slay this preconception of my own limitations then anything was possible. It might give me a path towards believing I was capable of all that was required of me.

DAY ONE

I woke with the sunrise and the sound of birds causing mayhem in the hedge and trees. I was no longer blundering through the land; the silence of sleep had helped it absorb me. The coolness of my face accentuated the warmth of the duvet and the mattress. I heard a brook rippling nearby I'd been deaf to the night before while the city still clung to me. The light shocked my lids closed and I squinted barefoot across the dewy grass, smiling towards the eco-toilet and shower block. Slightly alarmed to feel so human and free.

After I'd showered, bacon sat silently in the pan but nothing crowned the perfection of that morning cup of tea. The fact something I'd made in the same way as every other day could taste so different was a sign my conscious experience of the world had changed already. I knew I was well on my way. The geography of the mind fascinated me. The journey into the depths of myself required a new physical location, but after all those books I'd read, I wondered whether all paths I walked actually lay within me.

I smiled at the pleasure of the feeling of being away from normality, opened my notebook and looked up at the clouds, the tops of the trees and the sheep tearing the grass. I could see them and woods at the end of a field through a wooden gate, tied with orange twine. It rocked back and forth in wind I couldn't feel but could see. These were the foothills of what lay undiscovered in my internal landscape. Buzzards wheeled overhead. My pen hovered over the paper.

The car journey had started the process of acclimatisation and sleep had done the rest. The roads unravelled the identity I wore as I escaped London. Becoming aware of myself inside in that way you do when you are surrounded by countryside and people in service stations who don't know you. Road signs had prompted memories and faces from my life so far that smiled and frowned at me. It was the first time I'd realised I was old enough to have those kinds of memories. Ones with an emotional context and perspective on today rather than a static image of childhood, or the blurring memory of a memory. Wisdom collecting, and refashioning, the fragments of emotional entropy. I had begun to shed the various titles and descriptions I had collected over the years and was just left with me. I felt strong and fragile at the same time. Recognising what remained with a kind of knowing nostalgia.

I had given myself a prescription for the week that I knew would help me mentally. No screens for one thing. No morning weigh-in to see whether I'd gone over thirteen stone that week. No meetings. No emails. No investors. No being a CEO. No phone calls or voicemail. No being an employer or employee. The absence of this life thrilled me. Just wood, my hands, a teacher and me. Could I make it? And if I did, how would it change me?

I pulled my bike out of the car. Checked the brakes hadn't been twisted into uselessness in the boot and pressed the tyres automatically. All good. I had a shoulder bag with water, apples and biscuits and set off along the track to the main road.

A black dog dozed with his nose on the threshold of the Otter Surfboards workshop who stirred and snuffled at my feet when a familiar face came out to greet me, wearing a broad smile and an apron covered in dust and wood shavings. He introduced the dog as 'Buddy'. I don't know what I expected, but when James then hugged me to say hello we unspokenly agreed to pause our familiarity. I realised then the deal I'd made. He had me. He asked if I wanted tea and pointed at the wooden work table.

There was a saw with Japanese writing on the blade next to a flat template of wood with shapes marked inside it. He showed me how to cut one of the pieces, explaining that Western saws cut on the push but Japanese ones cut on the pull (this allows the steel to tense so you can have a much thinner blade) and left the rest to me. I seized his knowledge hungrily, but hung up my bag, wondering how to reiterate my hopelessness when it comes to making anything. I watched myself perform a dance of nervous self-deprecation, my eyes watering as I laughed into stupidity, but it stayed in my head, which surprised me. Didn't we both realise I would screw this up? I said nothing, realising at that moment the only thing I feared more than proving my incompetence was being irritating.

The walls were filled with saws, clamps, wooden detritus and shavings all over the floor. Wood in all its forms but most clearly, in those first moments, in the air. I smelled it before any other sense had caught up. I'd breathe it into my lungs all day every day, despite the offer of a mask, and by the end of the week I'd be wheezing and coughing merrily.

The shapes marked on the flat piece of wood were pieces of the surfboard's internal skeleton that had been machine-scored, but I had to cut them out and fit them together. The anxiety of screwing up was crushing at first. The poplar plywood was soft but every pull of the saw juddered until he guided the angle of my blade.

I calmed myself and looked around the workshop. My hands and arms rested on the table. Nothing was smooth. Dried glue, saw-dust and knots of wood gave every surface texture that I felt with my bare arms. It was a small workshop, with three tables where you could make boards on one side and some serious-looking machinery and saws on the other. At the back there were shelves long since bent under the weight of pieces of wood. Behind me, to the right of the front door as you looked out of it, was a rack filled with finished and incomplete boards and panels for others yet to be constructed. The pieces of mine must be in there, I thought. A small sink and kitchen area to the left of the shelves at the back would become familiar for making tea. Behind that a door hid a toilet, sink and boxes of bits and pieces and surfing magazines. My eyes fumbled with the textures around me. His workshop morphed into fractals as I stared into it. I blew away the dust while sawing as I increased in confidence. I saw frac-tals of depth in my conscious attention of the moment too. The sound and tension of the cut I felt through the saw was invig-orating and new. The knot of doubt in my stomach continued to loosen. Wood coiled from the blade. I paused to write in my notebook. 'It isn't being cut, it gives way like the ocean as you walk into it.' I smiled at the absurdity of such desperate poetry and put my notebook away. I was too keen. He sat on a bench drinking tea, smiling politely, watching me.

'Surfing is completely selfish,' he said unashamedly, filling the workshop with his voice for the first time since I'd arrived. Fold-ing his arms across himself in defiance rather than defensively. 'It benefits no one but me. But it makes me happy and that makes me a positive force in the world. I do very little harm, you see.'

I blanched as he said it. 'So you don't confuse suffering with virtue like everyone else in the world?'

His expression lifted. He smiled, and nodded. Wordlessly letting me know he was there for the same reason as me. It had taken my whole life so far to understand that was the root of my anxiety.

Once the pieces of the frame were cut out I sanded them to make sure they would fit together seamlessly. They were strong but tight, so pushing them together required nerve as well as a powerful thumb and finger delicacy. Just as I felt I was getting the hang of it, one of the pieces snapped when I tried to force it into place. The second before it splintered I knew it was happening but I was too clumsy to prevent it. I was jolted by panic. I had not believed him when he told me I could make a surfboard. Now I'd screwed up before I'd even begun. I had no chance. I felt the white heat of childhood humiliation. There was too little of my life left for the adolescent nonchalance I used to wear so brazenly. I realised at that moment how much it all mattered to me. He smiled and shrugged. 'We don't use that bit anyway.'

He tensed his fingers and popped the fractured piece out of place like a mother crocodile carrying her young in her teeth. His fingers were thick and the nails were chewed, which surprised me. I saw then the muscles of his hands had dimensions of knowledge and aptitude too. He had dried glue on his fingers, giving them a yellow hue.

I assembled the rest of the skeleton with nervous determination and evolving relief. Each time the pieces popped in together I felt my confidence stabilise. In one place the groove was too shallow to make the cross-section sit flush. He pointed at the chisels on the wall and I stared, waiting for him to nod and confirm which one but he had already walked away. Taking Buddy for a walk. I looked at the range of chisels, hoping for inspiration.

I tried to pull away from my internal dialogue of doubt and force myself out into the world. I had to pay attention and take responsibility in the workshop, drag myself out of the current of expectation my normal life always pulled me along within. I felt uneasy but more alert and gradually grew content in that state of pure attention. I took the piece of the spine to the wall to find a chisel that would fit in the gap. I selected one that seemed the right thickness and size and took it back to the table, trusting myself. Slowly and minutely at first, I used it to ease out a few millimetres until I could fit the pieces together. I pushed it in and then sanded the excess away impossibly slowly. Taking my time so as not to remove too much. 'You can take wood away but you can't put it back,' he had said. It became meditation. Calming and smoothing my nerves away.

I stood back and looked around myself again. My eyes kept spotting areas that were not flush enough for the top of the board to rest on so I shaved and sanded them meticulously. I realised then every inch of this board would be marked and changed by my hands. By me. I breathed in deeply, as though surveying a view from the top of a hill. I put the chisel back on the wall and knew in that moment I was different. I'd left the current of my normal life, my sense of what I was capable of, and was exploring a new course within, perhaps even outside, me. I smiled. Realising I was now inhabiting the space in his workshop my body was previously only filling.

I finished putting together the skeleton frame that would give the board strength, but in and of itself it was flimsy. No one would see this part when it was inside the deck but I took care over it methodically. Lovingly. I laid it out on the table as he told me about the base and top panels of my board and where they came from. 'A forest in North Dorset. It's self-sustaining. In the sense that they take trees at the same rate as new ones grow. It's a forest not a farm.'

Then he pulled out the base of my board from the rack by the door, which was the first time I saw the pattern of the wood. I felt excitement as I began to imagine what it would be like to have a finished surfboard, pausing to look at completed ones among other tops and bases. I expressed amazement at their beauty. He beamed.

It was one of his boards that had introduced us back at the Do Lectures in Wales. Before my talk he had given a workshop that I was too late to sign up for, but I stood and watched at the end, introducing myself as he packed his things away. For the first few minutes of our conversation my eyes had stayed on his board. By the time we made eye contact he was laughing at me. I couldn't believe anyone could make something so per-fect. So poetic. It was unfathomable. I had felt the contours of it with my hands, smiling broadly, and he mirrored me. Our hands read something in that board as though it were a form of Braille. Unsure about exactly what it was we knew to be real. But the board knew what it was. 1 + 2 = 3. Self-evidently the way it should be. It brooked no argument. The destination of the material, his eyes, mind, design, hands – all unquestioning. It was as though the combination of each had created some-thing exactly the way the universe had contrived it to be. Yet it wasn't uniformly machine-made. The thought that you can only achieve perfection in a frame of imperfection occurred to me.

Reactions like the one I had to the board were what I had been invited to talk about. The idea. It was about moments in life when you find things that speak to you for reasons you can't explain. Things like his boards. Objects, relationships, ideas that you know intuitively 'just are' the way they are supposed to be. Immeasurable constants in a world of apparent chaos and complexity. They were truths. I'd come to believe that profoundly. These moments of incalculable perfection were signposts you could follow all through your life. If you let them. But too few of us were aware enough to do anything more than stumble between them unconsciously.

The best way for me to explain what I mean is to tell you a story.

An estate agent was sitting in his office one morning when a blind man with a white cane walked in. The estate agent greeted him and the man tapped his way with the stick while feeling his way expertly with his hands and sat down in the chair. After exchanging pleasantries, the agent asked him to explain what he was looking for and began to compile a list of requirements.

The blind man described the number of rooms he wanted. The size of the garden, garage, the ideal location and so on, just like any of us would, and the agent began to make a mental note of some potential properties within the broad price range that would either fit these criteria or be close enough to be worth visiting. He finished his list after consulting with a colleague and took the man through the options.

The first viewing took place a few days later, but it didn't go quite the way the agent expected. He helped the blind man up the path and opened the front door. The blind man used his cane to find his way into the hall himself but, rather than continue into the property, he just stood there for a few moments before turning to the agent, shaking his head and saying 'no' and walking away. The agent was about to suggest going further in and looking around but stopped himself for obvious reasons. The blind man couldn't see. So they went to the next property.

They visited another four places that day and the same thing happened in each one. When they said goodbye later that afternoon, the agent said perhaps the next one they went to would be right, but the tone of his voice revealed his puzzlement was beginning to sour.

The agent found some other places and arranged to visit them with the blind man a few days later but the same thing happened in each one. The blind man just stood in the door for a few minutes before shaking his head and walking away. By this stage the agent was getting cross. On the third day, when they went to visit another three places, he began to look around to see if he was being filmed secretly, but he was too polite to say anything. He had never shown a blind person properties before. So he just carried on.

A week later a few new properties had been put up for sale so he took the blind man to those too, one before it had even been photographed. At this house, the eighteenth they had visited by this stage, something different happened. This time the blind man went into the door, stood inside for a few moments and began to grin. He nodded, smiling, turned to the agent and said, 'Yes, yes. This is the one!'

The agent was flabbergasted. He was completely baffled, and this soon grew into slight anger and resentment. This time the blind man did go further in but the agent could tell he had already decided. Everything unexpected he encountered, even the fact that it had one less room than he'd asked for, made no difference. He had known it was 'home' the instant he walked in the front door.

The agent's resentment disappeared then. He remembered all the other people he had ever shown properties to and realised they were just the same. Everyone had a long list of criteria their house 'had' to have but these lists were just a way to help them mentally prepare for buying a house. In the end they were all looking for the same thing the blind man had found in that property. We're all looking for the same thing when we rent or buy a place to live. Or rather we're not 'looking' for it at all. Everyone wants to feel 'that feeling' as soon as they walk through the front door. The feeling that tells you you just 'know' you are going to live there. None of us can explain why we 'know' it's the right place. We can't point to it in the walls or reveal it in the way the house is constructed. We 'just know' it's right, for reasons we can't explain. So the agent didn't say anything to the blind man. There was no point. He just smiled and helped him to the car.

This is the feeling I went to Wales to talk about. It's something I've spent the last ten years trying to understand because you don't just find it in the place you call home, although that seems to be where we're all most likely to recognise it. I've met machine enthusiasts who see it in everything from steam engines to motorbikes and lawnmowers. You can find it in all kinds of other things too. Shoes. Cars and guitars. Interestingly, a flat or house is the most expensive thing most of us will ever buy, so the idea we rely on a 'feeling' to help make this decision is worth pondering for a moment. I think we're all looking for it in everyone we meet and everything we buy and everything we do. It's what gives relationships meaning; we can all sense it in objects and ideas. I had no idea what it was, really, how it worked or why, but I knew it was real. Because every time I had listened to it, obeyed it even, however hard that was to do, the results always nourished me. And there was no doubt in my mind that this feeling was in his surfboards too.

I asked a friend who does semiotic analysis for brands to help them promote themselves more effectively what he thought of the idea. He understood what I meant immediately and said, 'Oh yes. It's my job to help put that feeling into things that don't have it. Through brands, marketing and advertising.' Perhaps this explains why consumerism often feels so disappointing. Manipulative, even.

I had delved tentatively into neuroscience and discovered that this feeling is entirely plausible in the context of how the brain works too. In as far as we can claim to 'understand' how the brain works, of course. The part of our brains that makes decisions has no capacity for language. It is separated from the part of the brain that deals with speech. This makes sense when you think about it. 'We' as a species had thoughts before we developed language so our consciousness will always be one step ahead of the things we say. Articulating our thoughts is incredibly challenging as a result. There is literally a gap between what we feel is right and how we verbalise the reasons for the choices we make. We often rationalise the reasons for a decision afterwards in an attempt to put our reasoning into words, but this is just a ritual we perform to try to make sense of our behaviour after the event.

This 'feeling' we all recognise requires a word, then, so we can call it out when we see it. I was told the word by a man called Andy I met while writing one of my previous books about machine obsessives. That 'feeling' you get when something you encounter in your life is perfect for reasons you can't explain is called *Spielzeug* and that was what had led, indirectly, to the founding of Unbound, the company I started with two friends. It's a German word that translates literally as 'play piece'. It is their word for toy, but it also has this other meaning. Something that is 'right' for reasons you can't explain. We have no equivalent word in English, so we should think of it and use it in the same way we use other German words like *Schadenfreude* and *Zeitgeist*.

James had listened and smiled. 'I know the feeling,' he said after I'd finished. He laughed in what seemed like relief. 'But it's not just houses, or things. I live in a landscape that has it. I live there because when I found it I had to stop and rest my feet.' I looked down and his feet were bare. They were bare now in the work-shop too. He never wore shoes. I wondered if he refused to have a barrier between himself and the world. We traded declarations in a form of enthusiastic Tourette's. 'I can see it in your board!' I had declared. 'You make it! You make things with it. It's only just occurred to me that the things that have it are given it in some way. By the person who makes it maybe?'

He'd nodded. 'It's what I'm trying to create. Every time I start with a new piece of wood, I'm looking to make something with that feeling you talked about. What do you call it again?' '*Spielzeug.*' He'd nodded and said it slowly, phonetically. 'Sch-peel-zoyg.' I watched as naming this concept – giving him a way of holding a previously unfathomable and nameless thing – helped him capture something that had always been floating in his mind and he couldn't stop smiling.

Now, in the workshop, he unearthed a wooden block, a template of the shape my board would have, from the back of the room. I screwed it onto the worktop with a drill so the frame could be glued and clamped on to it without it moving. This was the first time I'd ever successfully used a drill. I kept that to myself, though. The block was the kind of thing I imagined the Wright brothers used to build a wing. We wore gloves and carefully lay-ered polyurethane glue along the edges of the skeleton before clamping together the pieces I'd carefully cut out and sanded, using the block to support the upward curving shape. Once the skeleton was glued and dried, we put the base of the board itself on the block, marking in pencil where to glue the skeleton fast and then stuck it down with a mix of glue and wood dust that had the consistency of peanut butter. We clamped it all together using spars of wood that squashed it all in place, from one side to the other, with a layer of sponge between to protect the base of the board.

It was late afternoon when he called it a day. He could see I was exhilarated but only adrenaline had stopped me sagging. He saw the exhaustion that was about to hit before I did. There was no suggestion of the pub, or eating together that evening. He patted me on the back, pulled out a broom to sweep up the sawdust and sent me on my way. I heard 'sleep well' as I climbed on my bike and pedalled off.

I got back to the tent and was too tired to eat more than the scraps I foraged from my journey down in the car. I was still slightly overwhelmed by the assault of textures on my mind. My fingers felt tingly. Not painful, more the way your calf muscles do when you haven't been for a run for a few days and they are itching to take you somewhere. I looked at my hands carefully. Turning them and feeling the aching sinews as my fingers opened and closed, I realised how little I looked at, or knew, my own hands. I stared at them for a while. Almost apologising. They were waking up.

I searched my mind for thoughts and ideas and remembered the chisel and the portal in my definition of myself I had moved through earlier that day. My 'mind-forg'd manacles', as William Blake would say. I had found my route into the beginnings of a new way of thinking. Making something with my hands was opening me up. How I experienced time in his workshop felt different too. As though it held you like water rather than something that was either ahead of or behind you. I put that down to being outside my comfort zone. The day had been long but every moment like the twang of stretched elastic. A seamless procession of 'now'. I had been completely immersed in the smell and feeling of the wood. Cutting, cleaning, shaving, sanding. I had been so conscious of every new experience I was now completely exhausted. Being back at the campsite felt elemental too. Living along with the grain of the light and the wind. My focus on the wood and following the steps to make the board gave just enough structure to the day but there was inherent freedom for the mind to wander in it too.

I thought of the pieces of wood I'd begun to assemble resting in the workshop and the progress I'd made on that first day. I dared to believe I could do it. The next morning would require an early start as we were going to begin gluing on the rail strips that would become the edge running all around the board until they reached the top of the skeleton, on which the top could then be placed. I wasn't daunted, though, I realised with delight. That had fallen away at some point. It was like a walk. A walk with a rucksack on your back and a map in your hand, and I never doubted my ability to complete a walk. Even if I had never been where I was going before. I felt proud and eager. I had everything I needed. Where I lacked experience, he would guide me. I suppose I'd imagined I would help a professional make the board, and watch in awe, rather than actually do it myself. But it was already marked with me. I was doing it myself and my confidence was building.

A fresh bag of wood was leaning up against the brazier so I laid and lit my fire. Despite firelighters, it took an age and left my hands smelling chemical and wrong. I wiped them on the grass and that didn't help, but the flames were good to see. A couple staying in the tent behind me giggled over a bottle of champagne.

I wondered what they made of me. To be honest, *I* was wondering what I made of me. The new part of my mind that making the board had accessed felt calm, powerful and clean. Either that or I was just feeling ethereal through not eating.

I pulled a chair outside and stared at the flames, pondering how a single idea could have led me there, to that seat. How ideas and experiences could set your life on a path that changed your conscious experience of the world itself. How many new ways could there be of defining what I thought of as 'me'?

I had once stood in front of Monet's *Water Lilies* and understood this intuitively. No one ever says, 'Why did he always paint the same thing?' Because while they are all the same, they are all completely different. I realised, standing in that gallery, we're all painting the same thing. We're all living the same life, just from different vantage points, both looking out and looking in. Repeating ourselves and responding to our lives as authentically as we can. The story we tell ourselves of who we are becomes who we are. So we can change the stories that anchor what we tell ourselves we can become.

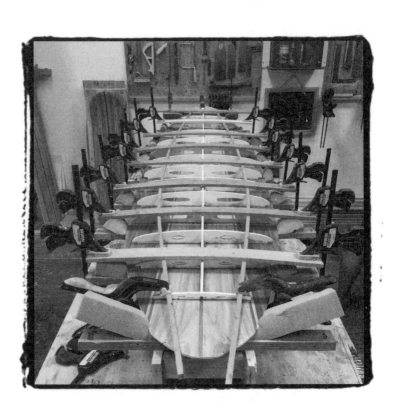

DAY TWO

My alarm went off at 7 a.m. I wasn't due at the workshop until nine but I needed a substantial breakfast after the scraps of a meal I'd had the night before and had been told about a truckers' caff nearby. I found a lurid pink temporary building that appeared permanent, with a red sign saying 'Smokey Joe's' on a side road off a commuter route.

A young, hassled woman in blue overalls suspended her grimace when I walked inside. (I imagined her face when her boss first gave them to her. 'I'm not wearing those!') She smiled at me and pointed to a table by the door. 'Be there in a minute, love. Tea?' I nodded. 'Mega mug, please.' Places like this always offered 'mega' mugs of tea. Barrels of life-affirming caffeine required by anyone whose job requires physicality. The table had laminated menus with every permutation of breakfast imaginable, headed by a warning that you were not allowed to change any of them. Whoever wrote the menu was revealing something deep about themselves there, I thought, and ordered ham, one egg, chips and beans and sipped the scalding tea. I didn't have the courage to ask for two eggs and no beans. 'Smooth Criminal' was playing on the radio and by the end of the song a platter of blazing hot food was in front of me. Truckers came and went. Smoking defiantly.

THE SURFBOARD

When I arrived at the workshop the same radio station was playing. James showed me a pile of rail strips and explained how long each one needed to be and to look out for tiny knots that would weaken the rail when it was planed and shaped later. They were eight feet long. I was not to use ones with knots under any circumstances. He told me to snap any I found into three pieces and put them in a bin by a huge circular saw so no one else would use them either.

End-on, the rail strips were like fingers of wood with the bottom cut through in a half-circle that ran all the way down and inside. If you planed one edge longways, so it was deeper on one edge than the other, it would sit flush, with the deeper side on the outside. This would curve up and inside the board, which was the desired outcome, until it reached the top of the skeleton. The rails started on the base of the board and were laid on top of each other – seven on each side in total – to curve the sides up to form the edge on which the top would sit. They were so flimsy that when you held them up, the far ends would sag to the ground despite being taut in the middle. Each rail had to be drenched with boiling water so it didn't snap when you bent, glued and clamped it into place. Eventually they would be shaped and sanded together into an entire consistent edge.

He helped me with the first one to show me how it was done, holding the long rail above a plastic bin and carefully pouring water from a steaming kettle down the bottom half, switching it over when one end had been warmed. Each rail took ten minutes to select, plane, bend and clamp into place along the entire length of the board, and another twenty minutes for the glue to dry before you could put on another one. I would spend the day alternating between one side of the board and the other. Fourteen rails meant seven hours. I was braced for a long day.

He was by my side when I chose the third rail, having now stuck the first ones on each side with his guidance. Under his glare I froze slightly, but he just waited for me to choose one, saying nothing to hinder or help. One edge was flakier than the other so that was the edge I planed. I had to do it at an angle and thin shavings began to appear behind the blade. I got more confident and pushed down harder. He told me never to put the plane blade down on the bench. I nodded. A touch on the shoulder told me I'd taken off enough and was done.

We removed the clamps that held the first rail while it dried and I measured the length of another alongside the board, being careful to avoid all the clamps that were holding the second rail down on the other side. I marked the centre of the board and the centre of the new rail with pencil so I could match them up. Then I rested it on the board before taking the glue and running it along the top of the previous rail. 'Use it sparingly,' he said. 'You'll find out why tomorrow.' But I was too concerned about it not sticking and it poured out. I darted forward to spread it along the top edge all the way along and it slipped down one side and then the other most of the way to the end. Speed was important now. I took the rail and placed the centre in place, bending it as I pushed it down along the one below. There was a pleasing acceptance as I did so, while he followed behind me clamping the new rail into place at the other end. When it was done I breathed out and smiled a 'phew' but there were plenty more to do.

The fact he was letting me do everything made me think there was a margin for error in each step, but the more I did, the more I realised it wasn't 'error' necessarily, just room for expression within a pattern or framework. I started to see that the journey to make the board was not, as I had thought, an exercise in comparing my ability unfavourably to an imagined version of perfection. 'Perfection' didn't exist. It was not the desired

outcome. The notion of 'perfection' spiralled off into thoughts about how many other areas of my life I'm restricted in by this unhelpful and limiting perspective.

That morning he taught me wordlessly, with a guiding hand or a raised eyebrow. It wasn't affectation, and felt as though he knew I was under some kind of spell. He gradually withdrew as I made progress. Appearing to guide with a hand or a bit of advice. He used words so sparingly that each one landed. When he said something, I knew I'd gone wrong and often corrected myself before he'd actually pointed out the mistake. I could tell he liked it when that happened. When I'd got to the third rail being clamped down on each side, he suggested we stop for lunch and drove us down to the beach I'd found on my first evening. We parked between the water and a café. His feet were defiantly bare. Buddy put his head in my lap the way he must have usually done with passengers but, after being bitten by one as a child, I've never been that comfortable with dogs, and I sat through the short journey slightly uneasily.

When we got down to the water people nodded to him, which he responded to by smiling and holding up his hand. We sat outside despite the cold and watched the waves. I was the first person who'd come to him to build a board who had never surfed before. I could tell this caused him some curiosity. The language he usually conversed in would fall on barren ground. We talked about nothing for a while and watched the sea. Seeing ourselves reflected in each other was disconcerting. We'd declared friendship in Wales so affectionately that we were now both slightly embarrassed. All I could do was think about the words I couldn't seem to say.

So we spoke about life in general terms. I blurted out the story I had settled on to describe my life so far, wondering as I told it

whether even I believed the narrative of it any more. But I talk too much when I feel out of place. There was always a disaster that led me to change my life. That was my narrative. Lone man fighting against the odds, even when those odds were 'mind forg'd' as often as caused by outside events. I had redefined myself three times in my life, I said. Started from scratch. And each time used rock bottom as a trampoline. That was one of my favourite lines. 'Rock bottom is a trampoline.' I used it all the time. Disaster seemed to sate me. Reassure me. I performed this speech to a therapist once, who said, 'Why do you have to wait for rock bottom? Why do you wait until it gets that bad before you act?' She suggested I was reassured by disaster because I felt deep down I didn't deserve to be happy or succeed. Rock bottom had become my comfort blanket, and the more success I had, the further I got from rock bottom, the more unnerved I would feel. She said that's why every time I'd had successes I'd changed tack and not allowed myself to build on them. It was like I wanted to fail. I disagreed, telling her I just got bored every eight to ten years and liked trying new things. She smiled and shrugged wistfully.

James told me how he had ended up on the coast of Cornwall making surfboards. His father had told him to make sure he spent his life doing something that mattered to him. So he went to university in Plymouth to be near the waves. It was the kind of thing that most parents would berate you for doing but it made more sense than anything else I have ever heard, sat there by the beach. He learned how to build furniture, but once he graduated he discovered he would spend most of his time as a carpenter, hanging doors. There were only so many you could do. So he built his first board as an experiment. He'd never looked back. Money was tight. But I could tell he knew he had what mattered, even though I got a vague sense he didn't quite believe it at the same time.

A woman in her mid-twenties with swept-back brown hair and brown eyes came to collect our plates. I imagined a forlorn beauty itching to escape from this out-of-the-way seaside town but that was my daydream, not hers. She asked if we wanted anything else and we both smiled 'no' as she walked away. I had a pang for my love at home. 'What amazes me,' he said, out of nothing, 'is that you're building a surfboard you may never use.' He laughed and shook his head. I went to defend myself but the expression on his face revealed he hadn't used the word 'amaze' to hide disdain.

After wanting to ask this question as soon as I'd arrived, I finally said it out loud. 'Has anyone ever failed to make one? Has any-one ever screwed it up?' He shook his head and laughed. 'You can do this,' he said, his voice changing to an unquestionable solidity. 'You can. Just trust me and listen. You're doing fine.' I smiled but needed more reassurance.

He sighed, and then gave it to me. 'Only one person has ever nearly failed to build a board with me, but even he got there in the end.'

I said nothing but began to imagine the humiliation of being the first to fail. His face grew a broad smile while he waited for me to catch up.

'And he was a carpenter.'

I blurted out, 'What?'

He glowed. 'He was a carpenter. He was over confident. Too familiar with the tools. He went at the wood ferociously. I had to teach him to slow down and show delicacy. I nearly got to him too late on the final afternoon when he was shaping the top of his board. He was millimetres from going right through to the inside. I had to put more fibreglass on it at the top where he had planed too deep.'

'But . . .' I trailed off. He stood to leave and beckoned me to follow him back to the van. 'Now you need to do four more rail strips each side before you go home tonight.'

On the way back in the van he looked at me strangely and then asked the question I got a sense he had been wanting to ask since I'd arrived. 'You're not here for a board like everyone else who comes to see me.'

I agreed.

'So what are you building exactly?'

I laughed and stared at the road ahead.

We got back to the workshop and he walked Buddy while I selected my next rail strip. Checking there were no knots and then planing down one side so it would knit neatly on top of the previous one. I felt I'd earned my apron by early evening, with six rail strips done on each side. Clamps stacked up on the desk around the board and the glue began to expand between each one like bubbles on a badly iced cake. I thought with horror I might have to remove the excess at some point but dismissed it because no one would ever see the inside. I was two rail strips short but I was spent. He said I could go if I came in early the next morning to catch up.

When I got to the tent that evening I pulled out a handful of snapped, knot-covered rail strips that he had given me to use instead of the chemical firelighters. He also gave me a handful of wood shavings from the floor to get the kindle going. I got to work, sitting on the grass. The flames leapt.

I cooked pasta and pesto for tea, bought just before the shop in Porthtowan had closed for the night, and drank a warm beer. It was colder than the June evenings of my imagination, but comfortable sitting next to my fire, swallowing lugs of the fizzy Mexican brew. I hadn't planned to drink but being outside my normal life, even only for a few days, I could see alcohol usually bore the burden of being a reward or compensation for a recent negative event and amplified my gloom accordingly. But there at the campsite there was no immediate burden. No gloom. Sitting by that fire, a beer was just a beer. My perceptions drifted over to work. The reason I was there. Staring at the flames in the now mizzling rain.

I had never expected to start and run a company. I always say I did it by accident, or mistake maybe. The reality is that like a lot of entrepreneurs I had no choice. I lost my livelihood overnight and had to do something to pay the rent. Because of a mixture of my unconventional personality and certain undiagnosed mental health issues, I had failed to finish two stints at university in my late teens and early twenties. Now, on a CV that might look bad, and the people around me were certainly concerned about which path into life this would force me to take at the time, but the truth, I discovered, was that this lack of safety net actually protected me. If I had had a degree to fall back on when my working life unravelled, I would have taken one of the unsatisfying but perfectly reasonable jobs the employment agency could have offered me. But my lack of any qualifications, apart from two mediocre A levels, meant there was no 'safe' option available to me. When the idea that became Unbound emerged during the lunch hour that day in Bognor Regis, there was no reason not to go for it. Even full in the knowledge that

I had no idea what I was doing and would have to fake it every single day.

At the time lots of tech companies were trying to disrupt legacy creative industries. They were trying to shake off the bureaucracies that had calcified the artistic endeavour they had originally been built up to protect. My previous decade as a writer had given me first-hand experience of that. With Unbound, we set out to evolve publishing and bring authors and readers together by building a crowdfunding platform that allowed them to decide which books should be made. We had massive ambition and I dared to wonder whether we could build a business with a different set of values too. If the three of us were going to run a company, it would have to have a distinctive attitude. Could we build an organisation that stood for something? Might we actually change the world through a business? And could we run it in our own way too?

In those early years the scale of what we were trying to achieve was so far off it didn't feel daunting. I'm not sure I believed we would pull it off but that didn't matter somehow. We were three friends with an idea and we were having fun. My life became a to-do list, with new items appearing more quickly than I could cross others off. It was always so chaotic. We raised our first investment over a breakfast meeting and built the first iteration of the site to get us to launch the following May.

I did endless pitches and events talking up the company. Until we had built something worth believing in, as CEO I had to make people believe in me. That is how you raise money. But the tension between who I was, what I cared about and building a successful company had already started to niggle me. I found myself wrestling with who I was and who I needed to be. I was faced with levels of stress I had not encountered before. Having

spent the previous fifteen years as a self-employed writer, no one other than my immediate family had relied on me. Now everyone's jobs and the viability of the business were entirely dependent on me raising money. An investor said to me very early on I had three jobs. I had to have, set out and sell the vision of the business. I had to make sure we never ran out of money and I had to hire people who were better than me in every role.

In the first year we hired three members of staff to work alongside the three founders. Our first office was a pub where we still get mail occasionally. Authors were frighteningly happy to come there for meetings. It was anarchic, instinctive and took place in a kind of well-meaning, alcohol-driven haze. We had our first major success at the time but we were still nowhere near profitable so I had to sell more equity. I found myself spending more time talking to investors than staff, something I still juggle with today.

I realise in retrospect I was contending with my preconceptions of what I was capable of as soon as Unbound began. I spent a part of each day sidestepping those preconceptions, trying to pretend the numerous limitations buried deep in my psyche would never have to be challenged or overcome.

DAY THREE

I got to the workshop at eight to catch up on the rail strips I was supposed to have done the night before. I took off the clamps and began to realise I had used far too much glue. It had erupted overnight all over the rail strips, on the outside, top and inside of the board. I couldn't leave it there. No one would see it but I would know. It had a kind of plastic sponge consistency. I began to pull it away with my fingers and then tentatively used a chisel, which was unnerving. The glue had to go, but not the rail strips themselves. It took an hour of methodical, slow, careful scratching to get rid of the worst excess. It was cold outside but I was sweating. By the time I had finished, the inside of the board was filled with clumps of glue. I grabbed handfuls and dropped them on the floor. At either end of the board the rail strips from each side crossed over each other and were a glued tangle, darting off the edge of the worktop. It was messy and muddled but you could tell what lay beneath. By 10 a.m. I had caught up and was drinking tea while my final rail strip was drying, clamped into place.

He rubbed his hands together. 'Right, now we need to put the nose and tail blocks in place.' I looked at each end, fourteen strips spiking off and entwined with each other. There was no room. I stared at him perplexed and he handed me a pull saw while explaining the technique I would have to use to cut off the ends of the rail strips and ensure I didn't cut through the skin of the board itself. After waiting for the final rail strip to dry, approaching the board with a saw shook me off balance. I drifted back into the current of my preconception of what I was capable of doing.

He took me to one side and showed me the technique again, to pull me back into the workshop. I would cut downward through the rail strips so the top six fell away, and go as far down as I dared on the seventh, and then cut parallel to the board to meet the downward cut, twisting my hand and therefore the blade away from the skin of the board as I sawed. A thin layer of glue and seventh rail would remain. He pointed to the chisels. I carefully etched the remaining pieces away so the nose and tail pieces would sit flush on its surface. I had to ensure I was always pushing the chisel away from myself along the surface to clean the excess rail strip away, using my right thumb to pressure into the wood, not the whole hand and never down into the board itself. Initially I fumbled as I tried to translate what I knew I had to do in my mind into my hands and fingers. All I could feel was another absence at the edge of my brain. It took a while but the 'feel' came slowly and my mind began to relax as my hands performed as I wanted them to.

This all required deep immersion into the texture and resonance of the board. I fell into the kind of trance you get listening to music, or very occasionally, writing, when you look up to discover an hour has gone by.

As I stepped away, with the excess pieces of rail around the board and chiselled fragments on the floor and all over the inside, I realised that at some point between this morning and lunch-time what had been a collection of bits of wood that had been cut, shaped, glued and clamped together had suddenly become a surfboard. Like all such intangible moments, I hadn't noticed exactly when the change had taken place, only after it had happened. I pushed away the pieces that had fallen on the bench onto the floor and took more handfuls of shavings and dust from inside the board with an absurd sense of pride. I stuffed a few rail offcuts into my bag for my fire later without thinking. I stood away from it and stared, smiling. It wasn't finished, the top wasn't even on, but it was a definitely now a surfboard. He patted me on the back and we broke for lunch.

Buddy made himself comfortable on my lap again. I felt the muscles in my legs relax a little. I was in the van but my mind was still traversing the surface of the board, trying to work out what was so 'board-like' about it all of a sudden. Remembering the grain, the feeling as I closed my eyes and running my fingers along the rail strips, feeling small knots of glue I would have to remove. How had its 'board-ness' crept up on me so soon?

When does anything become what it is? I wondered. The board was now a 'board' but it wasn't fixed. It wasn't complete. Its 'board-ness' would continue to evolve throughout the rest of the week. So how had it become one that morning? Even if it broke one day in the future it would still retain its board-ness. I thought of myself and all the roles I have in my life. All the versions of myself I had to live and perform. When did I become each of those things? Was I each of those things yet? Was I capable of continually evolving into each role? Was I fixed? Was I a success? Would I ever be complete? Eventually my thoughts caught up with the motion of the van.

I broke the silence as we drove into town. 'Autotelic.' He looked surprised. 'Have you heard of it?' I said. He shook his head. 'It's someone who does something purely for its own sake. I think sensing *Spielzeug* in something tells you the person who made it is autotelic and the thing they make proves it. I think you are. Autotelic I mean. And that's why your surfboards have *Spielzeug*.'

He looked as though this was the most normal thing in the world for me to have said and then did what he so often did, in retrospect. He batted my question back. 'Are you,' he paused, 'au-to-te-lic?'

I looked ahead at the road; he drove fast in that way people who live in the countryside do, using narrow lanes as flumes they can pour through. 'I want to be,' I said, holding the dashboard as we surged around a corner, raising my voice above the screaming engine. 'But I don't live for the sake of making things like you do. I'm trying to work out the answer to that question I suppose.' My voice almost shouting.

'What about in your writing?' We topped a hill and the engine calmed. He was formal, intrigued. 'Or your company?' He glanced at me.

I shook my head. 'I don't know.'

We sat inside the café this time. He asked me more about my life and we talked about Unbound. Five years on we had been getting a lot of attention from potential acquirers and venture capital funds. Later that year we would need more money to continue our expansion. The next round would be a big step up. It would mean planning a presence in America. I had started the company by accident and done a decent enough job until now. But I wasn't sure if I could continue to evolve within it. Could I raise another round of funding? More importantly perhaps, was I ready for what successfully raising the next round of funding would mean? Was my ambition and the stress, exposure and uncertainty it entailed really compatible with the daily life I wanted to lead?

'You're the CEO, though. That sounds impressive.'

I laughed and told him the truth. In the start-up world you are called CEO long before you actually are one. But everyone wants that title. Mark Zuckerberg's first business card at Facebook said 'I'm CEO . . . bitch!' on it because the job title meant he'd arrived. I read somewhere that starting a company today is a bit like what forming a band used to be. I agree up to a point. The CEO is the lead singer. There's a perception that you are disproportionately more important than other members of the company even if in reality – in terms of who and what is required for the business to succeed on a daily basis – that isn't so. If it was your idea, or your co-founders agree you should lead the company, then you are given the job title, often in lieu of getting paid. Everyone around you – co-founders, investors, your staff – knows you haven't a clue what you're doing at the start. They and you all know it's nonsense. But it's a necessary nonsense. 'Fake it till you make it' is the mantra and it's a good one.

In the early days people have to believe in you until you have built a company worth believing in. Some will back your potential and invest money to make that happen. Once you've raised some money you *start* to become an actual CEO. But there's still a long way to go. If you can get this far, you become a kind of pseudo-leader. The further you progress, the more you realise it is not what you thought it would be. Like everything, really. At that point you have to make the transition to become the actual ruler of your company. You do this by changing the perception of yourself in the minds of those around you by the way you behave, which means you have to actually change the way you perceive yourself first. This is a massive thing and where most people fail. Changing myself is what I spent most of my energy on. Your reward if you manage it is to become a kind of dad figure everyone needs but also slightly resents. Even your co-founders.

By now you are beginning to realise you will have to continually grow as a person if you're going to make the business a success. Your skill set has to evolve. Fast. And by this time your business is a few years old and you realise you have an actual business to run and what that means. The early excitement fades and it becomes more about processes. You go from a handful of employees to ten, then twenty and we'd now got as far as fifty. The most senior people around you want to be the one with your 'ear'. The sole person you trust, rely on and tell everything to. They unconsciously jostle for that role all around you. If you can get through all of that without alienating any of them, then you might have earned the job title. But at that point, now your hair has gone grey and the key relationships in your life have been tested, and you've learned how to placate people, dealt with well-meaning advice you have to listen to but not always act on, made sure the business has enough money, hired people who are better than you in every position – effectively handing power over to others in specific areas of the business at the precise moment you first begin to actually deserve that power yourself (which is a very hard thing to do) – once you've got through all that then you actually are a CEO.

You'll know because you'll have realised there will never be the moment you were aiming for when you started. That point when you could sit back and relax and know you 'did it'. The 'plateau of certainty', as I had come to call it, that you were motivated by all along turns out not to be true. The constant uncertainty that drove you to reach this plateau *is* the plateau. That nervous feeling in your stomach you can't remember not feeling won't go. You think having raised money and removed the immediate threat of going out of business would give you a rest from that feeling, but no. Because you realise all those things you said you would do if you had the money now need to be actioned. So the feeling never goes. It's your new reality. The plateau is learning to live with that ever-present feeling and not letting it bother you. Once you realise that, you can call yourself a CEO freely. But guess what? You don't care about your job title now. And that's when you know you really are one. When you see it for what it is. You no longer see whatever other people see when they see those three letters together. Because you know.

At this point I trailed off but James stayed quiet. I felt I had failed to explain it properly.

'Have you ever said a word over and over again out loud so many times that eventually the word seems to have lost its meaning somehow? It's no longer a word and is just a sound? You pronounce it differently and it doesn't matter. Whichever way you say it it has lost its meaning. Even though nothing about the word has actually changed? Well, the realisation is kind of like that but metaphysically, I suppose. It's a bit of a slog to be honest, and by the time you've "made it" it no longer seems to mean what it did when you began.'

He looked severe. 'Is that what you're looking for? Do you want to leave the company?'

I looked up at him across the vinyl table, over to the bowl of water Buddy was drinking from by the cutlery drawer at the back of the café. I let my thought processes dissipate before voicing a reply, and sighed.

'Sorry. That was a bit of a rant. I think I needed to say it, though. Thanks.'

He urged me to continue with a raise of his eyebrows.

'I do want to leave sometimes. But it's so hard to get this far and once you have, it's hard to leave. So many people are counting on you. Relying on you for their job. And it *is* fun. I'm a different person now, that's for sure. And I only became that person because of what I've done. I'm happier in my own skin. I've met so many extraordinary people as well. And I only got to meet them and have inspiring conversations because of those three letters after my name. I was invited to the Do Lectures because of what I had achieved with Unbound. Not directly, perhaps, but my job title is a sign there is something about me that might interest people more than my name would alone. It's similar as a writer. Being called a "writer" or "author" gives you status that other people seem drawn to. It's a filter, you could say.

'But the main thing is how doing this has made me change. When you start and run a company from nothing, every weakness you have is put under a microscope. You either have to deal with those weaknesses in yourself or you will fail. You'll either get fired, sidelined if they can't fire you, and then replaced, or you'll drive the company to ruin or burnout. I've come to see running a company as the greatest self-improvement exercise you can go on. It teaches you who you are, and who you are capable of becoming. I like that aspect, because that is what it means to live. To grow. But it's tough to grow all the time. It's grinding to be under that level of self-scrutiny.' I stopped, aware of the 'First World problem' nature of what I was saying. 'I mean, I've done worse jobs. Jesus. And ones with much, much worse pay. But this journey into myself, or I'm beginning to think out of myself potentially, is what makes it interesting.

That's why I don't quit. Because I actually love it. Maybe it's Stockholm syndrome.'

I laughed.

'But I'm learning to be different. In a good way. And I believe profoundly in what we're doing. What we do is worth dedicating my life to. But the constant need to push myself, to challenge my notion of who I am all the time. It's all-consuming.'

'Until it really works and you sell up for millions of pounds?'

I scoffed. 'Yes, that's what it's supposed to be about. Money. But I have worked out your "exit" is not the money you may or may not get at the end. I have at least realised that by now. If you want it to mean anything at all then your exit has to be every day doing it. I've met people who sold their companies and now have literally hundreds of millions of pounds. Some of them are in bits. They don't know what to do with themselves. They are so angry but they don't know where to aim that anger because on paper they "won" by getting out. That idea of an exit is profoundly dangerous metaphysically. This is the language of business, though. It's really odd when you start to analyse it. The language of war and conquest. It's very last century.'

The door opened and two bedraggled surfers came in laughing, one of them rubbing his hands and face with a beach towel. Their voices boomed with energy. They called over to James, who waved and said hello. One of them went to the counter while the other sat in the corner by the fire door. It had a green EXIT sign above it.

I pointed to it. 'You only ever usually see that word above an emergency escape route. But in my world the purpose of running a company is supposed to be your exit. Isn't that telling? Why would you do something if the only purpose is to find an emergency exit out of it? I've never understood that.

'I'm not doing it because of that definition of an exit. No. My exit is how I evolve personally. The tangible sensation of realising how much I've learned. It's hard to notice it yourself, because you are in your head the whole time. Like watching yourself age. You can't because the change is incremental. But you can see what you've learned and how you've changed in the eyes of the people around you. In the way other people start to look at you. That's the challenge. I've met entrepreneurs who have got out but who see the money as a side issue. I'm not naïve, I've never met a rich person prepared to give all their money away – even philanthropists stay in their very nice houses and keep their luxury holidays. I'm not saying the money is irrelevant, but what they really get out of it is what they learn and how they change, which they then want to use in the world. Because they've gained a different perspective. An inner confidence. That's the exit I'm after. I don't care about the money I may or may not get beyond living a comfortable life, like the one I have now. No one in my family wants for anything they need. So forget the equity stake. I'm interested in evolving as a person. That's what I mean when I talk about 100 per cent growth. Incidentally, though, the company only succeeds if you grow, so in the end it's all aligned.'

When we got back to the workshop he gave me the nose and tail pieces, two for each end, which he had made in the corner on one of his screaming machines. I would have to plane and sand them so they would fit together and then snugly in place. It took a bit of work to get them to fit and then we glued and clamped them to set.

Next came the box fins, so that in theory I could remove the fin the board used for stability in the water when travelling to and from the waves. This involved cutting and shaping pieces of foam and then sticking them inside the board where the fin fixing could go. The workshop filled with white dust as I hacked away. Next came the first bit of what I realised later was actual woodwork. Almost artistry. The top skin of the board needed to be glued on, but to make it fit I had to plane the top of the ribs flat so they met the original skeleton I had put together on my first morning. All the way around the board the surface of the ribs had to be flat to get a consistent surface for the top to be glued on to. To get the angle right I would have to plane away two thirds of the top rib and, as the ribs curved down, a half of the next and then a fraction of the third.

It took three hours, pausing when nerves got the better of me. I wanted him to watch over me and ensure every shaving I took off was OK. But he kept disappearing. Asking me to take responsibility. Once more forcing me out of the current of my normal life. I was alone in the workshop. Forced to concentrate. Planing away. Checking whether each section was flat with my hands, then moving up the rail to do the same, then coming back to check there were no lumps in between. As I pushed the plane forward, it took off more wood depending on the weight I put into each stroke; the weight changed as I pushed it away from my body and moved the downward motion from my centre of gravity. So I shuffled along, trying to keep the movements, and the amount of wood I removed, even. I watched the blade to check the thickness of what I removed was consistent, and corrected with more or less downward pressure when it wasn't. Sliding around the board, passing over it like a series of waves. He came in at the end. Ran his hands around it slowly without looking at it. I felt I'd done a good job. I tried to start a conversation but he was too focused. Then he stood at each end of the board and ran his hands from the tip down as far as he could reach on either side with his eyes closed. It took him a while to feel his way all around but he ended up handing me another smaller plane and telling me to go around it all again, spending slightly more time on areas he had marked with a pencil. An hour later we went through the ritual again. He made me focus on small areas four more times. Smiling.

I had been in the workshop for twelve hours now. I hated him. But I kept going. I felt childish resentment and frustration building up but I was old enough to recognise the bitter feeling meant I was learning, so I took it and carried on. When I was almost done I felt sorry for myself and paused to make a cup of tea but he stopped me and said he would make it, gesturing for me to go back to the board. I did as instructed with head bowed slightly. When he brought the cup over five minutes later, deliberately waiting – I knew even at the time – so I would carry on working, he told me to stop and walked around it feeling it with his hands again. This time he nodded. We drank the tea together in contented silence before he pointed to the vacuum cleaner in the corner. The top could now go on, but only once I had sucked away the shavings and glue from the inside.

I felt renewed energy. The top was going on! I picked away at any loose balls of glue and scratched the shavings away with the sucking tube. I struggled to get my hands and fingers under the rail strips to pick away the bubbles of glue and some had to remain. But when I was happy it was as clean as I could make it, he told me to sign my name inside. A surfboard is a work of art, he said, and all artists sign their work. I wrote myself a message that no one will ever see and signed my name slightly tearfully. I was tired, yes, but I had never signed something I had made before and already it felt 'Spielzeug-y'. The knowledge that inside the board was something no one would ever see felt like a bookend on my eternity.

We pulled out the top and sat it close by and then put glue on the top of the rails I had worked on so painstakingly. And on the nose and tail pieces and the skeleton from the first day. We lowered the top on carefully, making sure the design and grain of the wood matched up at each end. We clamped an end each and then checked each other's measuring before laying sponge strips across the surface and clamping spars of wood across each one. My board was hidden in a kind of pressurised scaffolding that would hold it all in place while it dried overnight. I smiled and hugged him. Holding on for longer than I intended. He waited until I let go before releasing his grip of my shoulders.

I cycled home slowly. Taking in the hedges and the gravel that collected on the junctions of the country roads. Looking up at the trees being blown around and the crows flitting about. There were potholes in the road and small passages in the hedges leading to the fields. I knew I had achieved something then. It was certainty of a sort. I was only part way through the process, there was still plenty of time to screw it up, but I realised, freewheeling down a hill to the entrance to the campsite, that I wasn't going to. I finally believed him.

I thought of Unbound as I unzipped the tent. Wondering what was stalling me. After five years running the business it was finally in a place where it had the potential to mean something. I looked ahead at what was on the horizon. I always looked at the business from various time-specific vantage points. Daily, weekly and monthly revenue levels to keep tabs on the pulse of the organisation, and then quarterly and annual performance compared to the previous ones and so on, but also the longer view. Where we were aiming for in terms of strategy. For that

you have to imagine years, decades ahead. But the most pressing issue was always the burn rate and the 'drop dead' point when you ran out of money. I knew it was only a matter of time before we needed another round of financing. Definitely within the next twelve months. We were pursuing a growth strategy. This is very common among technology companies. Get big as quick as you can and worry about profit later. Our business had solid underlying financials so we were not one of these increasingly ephemeral tech companies, but we are in a sector where the traditional players have been so slow to innovate that investing now could give us an edge in a multibillion-pound global industry. We were in the unusual position where growth was the sensible – as well as the bold – strategy. I was confident I could raise the money but suddenly it felt very different than before. Perhaps it was the political climate after the Brexit vote. Maybe something else was happening. But up until then raising money was a case of survival. It was that or face bankruptcy. This time the same rules applied but I knew it was also something more personal for me. I was struggling to work out whether I wanted what raising the next round of money would mean for me.

For a long time, perhaps my whole life, I have struggled to distinguish between whether I'm scared to do something or if I just don't want to do it. For years I thought this was something specific to me, but having finally got the courage to say it out loud to a group of friends, I was astonished to find everyone said they felt exactly the same thing.

DAY FOUR

I woke early to go running. I parked my car near the café we'd been to for lunch each day and walked on the beach to warm up. The wind battered me but collected me at the same time. Urging me on. I ran up the steep coast path I had walked up the night I arrived. I wasn't used to running up such a steep incline and was quickly exhausted, but felt invigorated by the wind and the light. Gorse nipped my ankles while wet grass kissed my shins and knees. I lost the path at some point, fearing it led too near the edge of the cliff, and ended up running inside and on the edge of a winding ditch. I opened and closed my hands and fingers as I ran. My God they ached. All that clamping and planing. I focused on trying to maintain regular breathing to keep going as my leg muscles screamed. On and on. When I had been going for fifteen minutes I stopped and then turned and headed back. The wind was now blowing into my lungs and it sated me. I smiled. This was what I needed.

Whenever I run it's always hard at first. I only feel the pain ease when I've been going for a mile or so and even then it's no less difficult, I just know by that stage I can do it. So I carry on. Despite the pressure in my chest. I can go for an hour if needs be. In ten years of running I have realised it never gets any easier. Not initially. Over time you learn to accept it. To keep going anyway. You run. But every now and then you get what I'd come to call runners' bliss. It has only happened to me three times. After half an hour or so you feel as though you could run forever. You are unstoppable. Tapping into hitherto unknown reserves of energy in a mental and physical state of self-awareness and confidence. It must be part of the *Spielzeug* spectrum, I suppose. A moment of pure insight. I would get one again if I kept going.

The eco-shower half an hour later was heaven, warmth pushing away the cold air around me. The run had done what it always does and my mental equilibrium was back in place. The positive impact instant. My tent was bathed in mist when I walked to it barefoot, hair dripping onto my shoulders. I looked at my watch. There was enough time for a quick visit to Smokey Joe's. I listened to Dinosaur Jr. as loud as I dared while riding towards my new favourite pink building.

It was a day of sawing, filing and planing, eventually merging the top of the board with the rail strips I had so painstakingly selected, worked and glued in place. Everything we had done so far was about strength and structure. That was no less true of the work we would do on the outside of the board but we were also finessing now. It would be a surfboard, so it had to be worked until it would glide through the waves. I thought of what I had written inside, grinned, put on my apron and embarked on the firm but delicate balance of filing away the top of the board on the edge until the top rail underneath came into view. It was a very rough file, and felt odd to use something so brutal to achieve something so refined, but I followed his instruction. Once I had ground it down all the way around I also had to plane the top of the board to have a uniform curved edge leading down from the flat top, where I would, perhaps, one day stand, to the now exposed rails. I grew in confidence and he urged me on, telling me I had to have confidence and trust my instincts. I was not expected to create a perfect finish now but to remove the excess wood so I could refine it all on the last day.

Once this process had progressed as far as required I had to work to merge the cedar top with the rail so you could see but no longer feel where it joined. This was my favourite bit so far because I knew precisely what I had to do, how to do it and had a visual clue if I went too far. I went absurdly slowly at first, hypnotised by the action of the plane and the coil of wood being removed. I became so accurate, ensuring precisely the correct thickness and colour of shaving was being planed away. The morning turned into early afternoon and I realised we'd had no lunch, and I hadn't actually seen James for what felt like hours. I put my head down and continued. Buddy bounded in ten minutes later and he was close behind, holding out a warm paper packet and a bottle of water as he came through the door. 'Chicken and vegetable pasty – we don't have time to go out for lunch today.'

The typically English, and by English I mean wet, mid-June allowed us some sunshine that afternoon. We sat outside wearing T-shirts and jeans, leaning up against the wall of his workshop. I slugged the water and bit into the crunch and then warm salty taste of chicken and gravy.

We talked about the board. He explained the top surface was important but the underside, which we would complete tomorrow, was where all the skills we'd learned that week would be required. I wasn't sure what skills I had that I would be using, but I had confidence I would know when the time came. I told him it felt like a kind of meditation, watching the coil of wood, a few millimetres of light-brown cedar and the same amount of the white rail each time. I was using a completely different part

of my brain, I realised, in his workshop than I did when I was working. He countered immediately, suggesting the person I was becoming running the business, through the rituals and artifice of my daily routine, was surely just the same process as finessing the board I'd spent all morning doing. I laughed and told him I hadn't considered it that way.

I thought of all the meetings, the ideas I talked about, the belief in what I was doing, the process of raising money as being a kind of methodical metaphysical planing. Eventually I replied to him. 'But even if that were true, how do I know what it is I'm building? You're here to tell me how to make a surfboard, but I don't have an equivalent of you telling me how to build a different kind of company. Or how to be a better husband and father for that matter.' He stood up, threw a stick for Buddy and walked after it, only looking back over his shoulder with an amazed expression on his face as if to say, 'Really?'

It was 3 p.m. when I went back to the board and immediately found parts I'd overlooked that needed attention. When he came back he had templates for the nose and tail, drawing around them with a pencil so I would know where to saw the excess of the nose and tail away. I cut around the line with a saw matter-of-factly this time, and got to work with the plane to turn the flat nose and tail into soft curves both underneath and on the top, creating a seamless point at each end. It was 7 p.m. before I left for the day. I held my head a little higher as I walked to my bike. I couldn't quite believe there was only one more day.

I bought fish and chips on my way home and ate it with my fingers as my fire began to catch light. My hands were so sore, my lower arms ached. But I was still smiling. I was aware of my life more deeply. I was throbbing. I thought of the aching feeling in my body and wondered whether all my stresses and strains in my day-to-day life were just a metaphysical equivalent of these physical, muscle awakenings.

My friend and fellow Do Lecture speaker Michael Townsend Williams sent me a YouTube clip once. It's only a few minutes long but in it a rabbi talks about how a lobster changes its shell. Lobsters are squishy creatures that live inside a hard casing. The question he poses is how does a lobster change its shell, and how does it know when to change it? The answer is that it has to find a safe place where it can remove its shell, obviously making it very vulnerable. Then it can grow a new one. It knows when it needs to change its shell because it feels stress and physical discomfort. It feels tight. It can't move; it's incredibly uncomfortable. Amusingly, the rabbi then suggests if that lobster could go to a doctor it would be given antidepressants to cope with the feeling of distress and it wouldn't need a new shell. This is not a glib denial of mental illness. The point, of course, is that this stress is also a sign of growth.

I realised when I watched the clip that I saw the physical discomfort after exercise as something to be proud of. A sign I was using muscles I didn't normally use. So the feeling of unease I felt at work was just me using new parts of myself too. Most of the time running Unbound I have felt like a lobster who needs to change his shell. It's a slightly nauseous feeling experienced by most people, whatever job you do. Perhaps stress was a sign of progress as I honed and toned my mind to each experience. Each learning. I felt a sense of pleasure and pride in the ache of muscles after running. Could I deal with what I thought of as stress simply by perceiving the impact of it in the same way? I never felt shame in being tired after physical exercise. I did not see it as a sign of weakness. I never allowed that feeling of physical discomfort as a result of pushing myself to spiral into feelings of self-recrimination, worthlessness, anger or existential gloom.

I knew the limits of and respected my physicality. Perhaps I just needed to look at the source of my stress and the capacity of my mind to deal with it in the same way. After all, each period of stress had resulted in me being able to grow. Looking back, periodically the company had been through these states of stress and growth too. Each difficult period resulted in practical and cultural change and our performance improved. Everything and everyone felt much more at ease.

DAY FIVE

I arrived at the workshop sad it was the final day but excited to see the board at the end. I knew I had poured a lot of personal meaning into making it. If I could make a surfboard with *Spielzeug* it would prove I had remodelled my perception of what I was capable of. I would have evolved the story I told myself I had the capacity to become. I hoped some of that would cross over into the way I saw my role at Unbound and help with the next phase of its evolution.

James gathered me into the workshop with a stern look on his face. 'Today is the day. If at any point you are unsure of what you are doing, you must stop and check with me.' He held out his palm in a 'stop' sign as he said it. 'We're working on the underside now, which determines how the board moves through the waves. This is the most crucial part of the whole board.' Inevitably I gulped, but did not descend into fear and self-loathing as I might have expected myself to earlier in the week. I knew I could listen. I had come to know something of the tools. I had the ability to work at different strengths with each one. I could be delicate and careful. I no longer found myself daunted by an imagined version of perfection I couldn't hope to live up to. I trusted the faith he had in me and heard in the firmness of his voice an expression of that confidence.

We flipped the board over and he began to plane the underside at the top to show me the pressure and technique.

'The board has to be both "in" the wave and "on" the wave, so it has to have a rounded surface underneath at the front to go through the water but the underside of the back of the board also needs to have a determined edge so it can sit on the wave. Halfway along the board you also have to make it blend seamlessly between the two.'

I worked on the front first, planing carefully to start with but growing in confidence as I got my eyes and hands 'in'. He was by my side watching, not doing, but keeping an eye on my progress, nodding occasionally and guiding my hands. Then he surprised me by flipping the board over and telling me to sand the top of the board for a while. He watched me carefully for a longer stretch of time than he had done so far. I asked if that was to get my hands working in different ways before tackling the final challenge of shaping the underside and back of the board. He smiled, but that could have meant yes or no. I took it as a yes.

Sanding was the most meditative aspect of the work I had done so far. It felt more creative. Unchecked. This was to reach the final finish before the board was taken to have the clear fibreglass covering applied. The feel of the sanded wood changing over time amazed me. The surface was already reasonably smooth but there were imperfections where you could see the slight channels made by the plane. All those had to be smoothed out.

It felt as though we only had half a day's work to do. The pace was slowing considerably. Or perhaps it was about creating an atmosphere of reflection. The in-betweens of time opening. My physical movements were slow but my mind was moving very quickly, leaping from one sense of meaning to another, drawing parallels between the way I shaped the board and the way my behaviour had shaped my life. All of a sudden I made myself 'look' for the smell of wood in the workshop, realising I had got so used to it I now had to consciously try to detect it in the air. That felt meaningful somehow. Tomorrow, at home, the smell would have gone. What else about my life had I got so used to I now had to force myself to experience it again?

I found myself settling as the sandpaper delicately shaved the edges and imperfections away. Then we took away the top of the table I'd been resting the board on all week and found a sling of carpet suspended underneath that the board could rest in sideways while I sanded the rails. He gave me three grades of sandpaper to work through, getting me to check with him once I felt I had completed a full circumnavigation with each grade before moving on to the next. This part was joyful. I felt in complete control. Moving to sandpaper meant the changes I now made were fractional but no less crucial for the way the board would perform. As before, I sanded only up as far as the pencil line he had drawn three quarters of the way down the board. The difference between the surface texture of all the work I had done at the front compared to the back gave me a sense of progress. After the finest-grain paper had been scraped across the board, the texture of the wood was so fine. It made me smile. I could close my eyes and run my hands over the board knowing all those individual pieces and the glue had been combined into one thing. There was no way of telling where the joins were. Or the different sections it contained. How it had been constructed. It was a balm on my hands as I ran them over it.

I thought of the words I used to describe myself – father, husband, CEO, employer, employee – and the individual identities I had constructed in the way I perceived them. I had to move from one identity to another inside myself as I switched between each one. Each one had a different personality and temperament that over the years I had cultivated, or potentially used as an outlet for different aspects of 'me'. When would I realise the craft of my life meant these words, these roles I performed, were unified by one thing? They were all just aspects of my character that made me. They were not in conflict, or they shouldn't need to be. I had to accept these moving definitions as the evolution of me. To accept the father and husband at the same time as being an employer, CEO and employee. I couldn't continue to fragment myself. They were all me. Perhaps this is what I needed to allow for in myself to build a different kind of company.

My hands were now rougher than the board. It could feel the calluses and scratches of my fingers and palms as it felt them on its surface. I thought again of the message I had written inside. When he was happy I had done enough, we placed the top back on the table and rested it upside down. After lunch we could work on the bottom. The final stage.

We didn't speak on the way down to the café in the van. He was waiting for me to say something but had sufficient patience, and was enough at ease with himself, for us to be silent. When we walked over to the outside table I looked around at the seasonal surf shops offering lessons with bright-coloured boards and wetsuits you could rent. Neither of us needed a menu. He went in to order two burgers.

He placed two bottles of water on the table with cutlery I knew neither of us would use. 'So . . .' he said finally, 'how are you feeling?' I laughed. 'Well, I don't think even I can screw it up now.' Then I remembered what he had said about the last bit before it was complete. I still had no idea how to work the part of the board that would sit in the water. My facial expression must have revealed myself and he started laughing. 'When are you going to realise you can do this?'

I was no longer sure whether we were talking about me being a father, a husband, running my company or building the board itself, but at that moment I understood it didn't matter. All were the same thing. They were just different vantage points of the same question. The reason I was there. The reason I did all the things I do. The acceptance of the alternative and sometimes paradoxical viewpoints that defined what I thought of as myself.

I tried to speak but felt stuck and just sat there pondering. In my head I have a comprehension beyond language. I now know it is the part of my brain I will spend my whole life interpreting because it has no 'language' of its own. I 'know' everything about myself intuitively in a way I can't explain, but the problems come when I have to communicate this knowing to myself and the world. I, we, are all seeking to be 'known'. Trying to decipher the thought processes, the experiences, the opinions we have in our heads, through communication, so we can be understood by those around us. But language is not enough. So we use body language too. And we use what we have absorbed from our cultural landscape that we're not even conscious of. But even the combination of all these things is not enough for us to be truly known. Sitting there I knew what I meant to say but had no idea which words I was going to use. The question was, is always, what distance would there be between the two?

But words finally came. Often I have images in my mind I can't see the relevance of but if I start talking about them they lead to a kind of sense. Or a narrative of some kind anyway. I saw my daughter's face.

'Olive is learning to do cartwheels at the moment. In the space of a few weeks she went from barely doing them at all to being able to do twenty in a row while we walked across the park. Now she can do a hundred. The first time she truly landed one she ran up to me and jumped up full of glee. I was filming her do it and the moment the filming stopped I captured her face smiling at me. In that frozen image I see her enlightenment and my own. I hadn't seen it happen consciously – her smile – until I saw the image on my phone because it happened so quickly. She had done something she couldn't do, which is important for her in myriad ways and is the path of all life. It is the bias of life to grow. To evolve. To do. Changing the perception we have of what we can do. Young children don't need to be told this, of course. For them the world is theirs to be known. But something happens to us as we get older and we begin to decide long before we've tried to do something whether we can do it or not.

'I think for me it was the shocking awareness of death that suddenly brought the daunting scale of adulthood to me. All of us glimpse the gap between the perspective of childhood and adulthood at some point for the first time and find it terrifying, even if not in such a dramatic way as it happened for me.

'In our early teens my friend Henry and I were kicking a football between us on the road outside his house when we were called over to a nearby house by his distraught next-door neighbour. There, in the garage, was the body of a man who had taken his own life. His wrist was cold in a way I have never forgotten. At the time Henry and I were big fans of the film *Stand by Me*, in which a group of friends go in search of a rumoured dead body, but the gap between my understanding of that film and this real-life experience triggered a torrent of unexpected emotions that instantly trivialised the movie. The stark intensity of that experience brought mortality home to me. I still feel as though my consciousness was paused at that moment in some way.

'But Olive is a long way from that moment, happily. She certainly tried hard for a long time to do cartwheels. She knew she couldn't do it at first, but because she is a child she kept trying and got better. She learned and now she has her reward. She can dance across the grass on her feet and her hands. She has taught herself what she can do. She has changed the perception she had of what she could do. And her face is pure bliss.

'I dropped my phone after she jumped up to me in the way children do. I held on to her as her arms gathered my head and neck and in that moment felt the sublime lightness of being a father. When your love for your child is that paradoxical truth of being limitless and intense but not remotely overwhelming.

'For me, in my life, the meaning of it also lies in the relationship between the two of us as well as her relationship with herself in that moment of triumph. In her smile and the knowledge that her smile is for me, her father, lies everything I require to live humanly. That is one of my moments of enlightenment. I love her completely. I live in fear of her being sad, ill or afraid, but those risks increase my capacity of love for her, do you see? I do not believe there is anything else as meaningful we have to learn or grapple with as a species. Pure love that for both of us is completely unquestioning, is our tranquillity, our unity. In feeling it while knowing at any point it can be swept away. Precisely because of its ephemerality.'

I paused self-consciously but he smiled. The sense of what I was trying to say began to dawn on me.

'But I am only aware of that moment because I happened to capture it with my camera. I've just this instant realised that my life is full of these moments. I am made entirely of these moments of experience but I just can't remember them individually because they happen too quickly. Moments with people I love. Moments of perfect love. Those moments are the narrative of my life. They make me who I am. Not the narrative of my preconceptions of what I am and could become.

'We all stop the frame of our lives in specific moments, often because of trauma or loss, and become frozen by those moments. They haunt us. They begin to define and restrict our sense of who we are. We revisit them over and over again. Noticing things in them, obsessing over them, and our response to the combination of the moments we focus on becomes the way we define ourselves. We remember how we felt when we remembered those moments rather than the original event itself. That's how memory works. You don't remember the original event over and over again. You remember what you remembered the last time you thought about it. Then you remember that act of remembering. Then you remember remembering the original act of remembering but no longer realise the original event is gone. Only our evolving construction of what we remember remains. So these are shadows of a fraction of a moment in a life full of other moments that for whatever reason we choose not to dwell on.

'I can see that making this board is a new moment for me and the value of it can't be ignored or warped in the act of remembering because it is a physical thing in the world. I can't remember remembering it and change the memory of the original memory because it is here. I can't corrupt it. I made it. It is here. Seeing it complete when I believed making it was beyond me will erase the moments – the memories of remembering – that instilled a false belief in my inability to make things.'

I took a deep breath and started to laugh nervously but he checked me with a firm look on his face.

'And *Spielzeug?*'

I paused, thinking. 'I believe that is one way of defining *Spielzeug*, actually. The physical manifestation of a moment of expression that you can't retrospectively question or manipulate. I don't mean you don't think it can be improved. I mean it is the perfect expression of the act of living itself. When you release yourself into something that exists in the world apart from you. But this is only one aspect of it. I'm beginning to think of *Spielzeug* as a spectrum of different experiences.'

I collected my slightly incoherent passion together again.

'I think *Spielzeug* is love. But a physical kind. Perhaps it's the actual love and appreciation of being fully conscious in time.' I paused again. Puzzling myself. 'I'm sure it's a way of worshipping time. Taking the religious connotations of the word "worshipping" away for a moment. Language has so much baggage but there is a semblance of what I mean in "worshipping". Perhaps the act of making something with love, for its own sake, being an autotelic, gives the thing we make a kind of meaning we can all recognise. That passes from person to person and from one age to another. It is a way of marking conscious time. Of defiance. Making these moments physical and undeniable. I can't pass over the moment of making this board when I'm feeling low. The self-realisation, the happiness, the confidence, is captured in it somehow in a way other people can feel. Its existence, my ability to hold it when it is done, proves to me my ability of what I can do that I cannot ignore and that others can also see. It is a moment of pure love that I believe in and that sets it firmly in my mind as a moment, defining who I am. It will become part of how I define who I am. This is the autotelic's path. I can't even surf, for God's sake. It's ridiculous. But that proves to me I have made it for its own sake. I mean it. *Spielzeug* is about marking who we are and making what we stand for real. In the world and not just our heads. The pre-language part of our brain where we "know" things but that can't speak for itself? I think things with *Spielzeug* are a bridge to that internal knowing. That part of our conscious existence. Taking those moments that define our lives out of our heads and making them real in the world. That's why we can sense it in physical things, because it reflects a part of us inside we know is meaningful and real that words will not allow us to capture. There are even theories that it was making things with our hands that led to the emergence of language. The part of your brain that is active when you use language is the same part of the brain that is active when you make things with your hands, so it must be all connected somehow. *Spielzeug*, being an autotelic, it's a way of us communicating what we most want about ourselves to be known. And we see this reflection of other makers in the things they have made that we encounter in the world. It's a form of language we make with our hands that words won't allow. It's in your boards. I've put it in my board.'

I stopped to let my thoughts settle.

'It's in art, music, maths and love. It's in shoes and furniture crafted for their own sake. It's in films and sculpture and books. It's in technology and engineering in cars and aeroplanes. But most importantly it's in how we define the concept of home. That feeling of calm acceptance. Where we can wordlessly merge with each part of ourselves. There is no place like home for a reason. And that's why we all enter the experience of *Spielzeug* through home. It's a doorway we've all passed through. It's existence itself. It's the one thing we can share that we all know.'

I waited, breathing so slowly it was as if I'd been meditating. He seemed pleased, which allowed me to continue. I had no idea where the words were coming from but they kept coming. A connection jumped across my mind that made no sense until I pursued it.

'I watched a documentary about space once. An astrophysicist was talking about time and said there is really no such thing as time. Our sense of time is rooted to the spinning of our planet on its axis and the number of those spins it takes to circumnavigate our sun. It's utterly meaningless to anything or anyone not on our planet. Our "time" is not "universal". We've invented it so we can catch a train home but it doesn't "exist" in the universe any more than a fictional character. So astrophysicists talk about time in terms of distance instead. The time it takes for light to travel *is* universal. But that makes no practical sense to us reading a book on our planet. In terms of the universe as a whole, "time" is therefore rather insignificant. The only universal law that relates to it in a meaningful sense is entropy. Decay. The universe and everything in it is falling apart. It will one day disintegrate completely so life, everything, becomes literally nothing. This sounds absurd but you can see this in the way we present evil in popular culture. Darth Sidious in *Star Wars*, the Dark Lord Sauron in *The Lord of the Rings*, Voldemort in *Harry Potter* – the religious Devil. What they signify is senseless oblivion. Entropy. That is the evil we cannot name. What will the Dark Lord Sauron do when he has crushed all life in Middle-earth? How do these masters of evil relax from all their deliberate cruelty? Where do they go on holiday to chill out? None of these questions are remotely plausible within the context of those stories because they are not characters who have daily routines, brush their teeth, wash their clothes and so on. They signify entropy. These characters frighten us, they make us shudder deep in our bones, because they represent all our destinies.

'Even religion offers no real sanctuary. If you believe in God the same rule applies. It just takes a bit longer to get to. What will you do in your heaven if it exists? What will happen when you've spent time with the people you loved in your life and met all your ancestors in your perfect eternity where they all reside? When you've met and hung out with all your historic heroes. Where will you go to escape your family when they drive you mad, when you've said everything you can possibly say in your heaven? When you've expressed love endlessly to them, it too becomes a word you have repeated so often it ceases to have any meaning. How will you cope with eternity then? When you've explored what feels like an eternity, you are exhausted with it all, the pursuit of sating your desires because they are all you will have left to explore. If religion is true, then curiosity, science, all the pioneering areas of human exploration we revel in have one simple and dull meaning. They are the whim of your God. Once you've realised this and examined all the worlds that are, have ever been or can be imagined, when you have done all of that and realised your time spent in your heaven so far is merely a millisecond, not even a millisecond, because eternity means never-ending so even the concept of a second is meaningless, where will you go in your mind then? You cannot escape. Is it too much of a stretch to realise that even if your God is true and your heaven exists in the end, you will desire oblivion too? There's no avoiding it. Even in exhausting the imagination of the human mind by following the concept of eternal life you will not stop the inevitable entropy of yourself. The decay of ourselves and our concept of the universe – of existence itself. All will end.

'*Spielzeug*, the autotelic, those moments of perfect love, of life, of meaning, me capturing the face of my daughter at the precise moment she did those first cartwheels, the feeling of home, changing the preconception of what you think you are capable of, the feeling of curiosity, runner's bliss – what these things represent is the battle of consciousness against entropy. They are the joy we hold on to in the inevitability of what we all face. As individuals and collectively as conscious beings. It is hopeless. We know we'll lose in the end but we don't care. Because you have to go on. And because love *is* enough. To have experienced life *is* enough. As long as you are not afraid to live, live with the bias to grow and grow beyond your existing shell. Living with the inevitability of oblivion, to have felt that, to have lived anyway and grown towards it, is courage and beauty beyond imagining. It's almost an actual heaven on earth. You might even invent this life – the mortal life – to escape knowing and experiencing what an eternal heaven actually means.'

I slowed down with realisation. I was stretching things now but my voice carried on.

'And this is the struggle I'm on. I'm struggling to make myself grow continually towards that inevitable moment because I know one day I will experience the precipice of my individual annihilation. There is a moment I am travelling towards when I will I gasp at the immediacy and potency of my final glimpse of life before I die. What will help me in that moment? What will keep me company on that journey every person who ever lived has either experienced, or will experience, so utterly and completely alone? I don't know why but I sense somehow the moments of love, life, spotting and creating *Spielzeug* are what will give me solace when that time comes. They will counter and hold me through that sense of being eternally, insensibly, alone. The business is the framework in which I am currently growing towards that goal. But I will outgrow it in time too.

'We create these moments in the business, actually. When you analyse it, as we have, you realise it's what we do. Every book

we publish has a story not contained within the pages themselves. The story of the people who wanted it to be published,
the author's struggle for meaning and to be known. We are all
autotelics in the company. We celebrate as conscious beings
the written word and the act of living itself. Liberating ideas
from the unknowable conscious human mind. Trying to put
them into words. That's the flag we're all running behind. Our
job is to bridge the gap between what we all know intuitively and
what we can explain. And this is why I love books so much and
have been drawn to them as soon as I discovered them. Because
when you read a book, the language, the voice, of someone else
is trying to access the language-less state of your own concept of
what is "known". To connect to you. Often it fails, but sometimes
– wonderfully, perfectly, beautifully – it succeeds.

'The thing I most love and value about reading is not the words
I read, it's what thoughts and feelings those words occasionally trigger in my own mind while I'm reading. The apparently
unconnected realisations that seem far removed from the book
but help me make sense of something in my own life. It's just
like that feeling when you run sometimes and feel you could
keep on going forever. It's a kind of reader's bliss. The ideas
that emerge to me while reading that are not written down but
the book has somehow pulled out of my mind. Those are the
moments when someone else's words find a way to enable us
to access our language-less state of knowing. They bridge the
gap briefly. Using metaphors and stories. But leave no trace.
You cannot explain the connection and the realisation you have
made and come to. Only that the act of reading made you feel
it somehow.

'You get writer's bliss too, when you write something and you
have no idea where it came from but it conveys your meaning
exactly as you meant it to. All writing, all art, the humanities as a

whole, are an attempt to bridge this gap between us. To connect us together and show us all we are not alone.'

James finished his water and looked out at the waves. I could tell he was thinking. He looked back at me and nodded. 'I think I get it,' he said. Deadpan. Then he paused and raised his eyebrows.

'It sounds a lot like surfing.'

We both burst out laughing. I felt the freedom and self-awareness of my own absurd attempt to communicate meaning. Accompanied by the catharsis of being heard but not having to take myself too seriously. The distance between what I meant and what I said was not as vast as usual, and that was enough for now.

Back at the workshop we ceremoniously turned the board over and began working on the bottom. He was fierce with me. This was the moment that mattered above all else. The hours drifted away in a state of harnessed anxiety. Each instant took all my focus and attention. When we were done, and he did help me this time, making much more confident and abrupt strokes across the wood than I had ever done, he stood back and sighed. I held up the board to see how the definition of the underside at the back had changed. We then both worked on either side three quarters down, swapping over after a few minutes, working the gradual change between the two.

It was not complete yet. He pointed to the orbital sander by the bench to my left and told me to finish the top and then to sand it all over again with an even finer-grade paper by hand. He helped me with the machine but after a while asked if I'd prefer to do it by hand. I nodded and he left me then.

I was vaguely aware of him tidying up in the workshop around me. I wasn't sure at first how long I should carry on but ended up zoning into the rhythm of sanding the sides, top and bottom over and over again. We didn't speak for hours. At first I assumed he would tell me when to stop, but as time went by I realised my final act of making would be to decide for myself when to stop. I had been sanding for some time with less and less vigour, having a conversation with myself, and eventually decided I was done. I felt a kind of contentment I had never experienced before, which words will not get close to describing, but the nearest I can get is a sense of buoyant finality. There was no anticlimax or wish to carry on. A kind of resonant peace. I couldn't stop stroking the board. Closing my eyes and letting my hands 'read' the surface. I found a few imperfections but was happy to leave them there because I knew years later I would still recognise them. I tried to work out where the week had gone as I scraped the paper across the wood with barely any downward pressure those final few times. How had I only been there for five days? I felt something new in myself. I had grown in confidence in a way I had never been so conscious of before. I would leave his workshop changed and self-aware of that change.

I put down the sandpaper and stopped. Stood back and called out to the workshop, without taking my eyes off the board and thinking of the words I had written inside. 'It's not just made of wood.' I paused as he approached. My voice cracking slightly. 'It's also made of me.'

He smiled, handing me a stamp that had his name on it with a pad of ink, and said it was up to me to decide if and where the stamp should be placed. I chose the middle of the top of the underside of the board at around head height. Then he gave me a pencil so I could sign it underneath before taking a soldering iron and going over my signature with it himself until my name was burned on the surface. It felt fitting the board would carry both our names and that we had marked each other's.

We had reached the limits of language now. We had long since passed the moment we were now aware had arrived. We hugged each other and this time let go simultaneously after a long time. He squeezed my shoulders before we separated. I was so happy. I felt tearful and slightly manic. Like I couldn't let enough light into my eyes. We talked about the practicalities of the board being covered in clear fibreglass and when I might come to collect it in a few months. But I stumbled over my words and was already mentally somewhere else. As I was leaving someone arrived. The swell was up. They had to go. He grabbed his board. I saw a childlike glee in his eyes.

*

I drove home to London in a distracted state of mind. I missed the board immediately and didn't want to move away from it. I was almost in grief. As though all I had learned might still be set within the rails and frame. But I was being pulled along by the gravity of those I love and that is always stronger than my anxiety.

Isobel opened the door at home and her smile enveloped her eyes. Her belly enormous but perfectly tight as she waddled the door aside.

I never imagined it would take me over a year to return to Cornwall.

ONE YEAR LATER

The following summer I finally carved out the time to pick up the board. I was in Cornwall for a family holiday, having got back a few weeks earlier from New York. I had gone there with John, my friend and co-founder, to test the water about launching Unbound there.

It had taken seven months but the fundraise was now done on terms we could accept. Although, to be candid, I feared the process had pushed me to the edge of sanity. But with money in the bank to fund the next phase of our expansion, the business had already shifted up into another gear. In both ambition and practical terms. We had hired new people with new approaches who brought extraordinary energy and ideas. They came reflecting a perception that showed me the company had evolved once again. We were all getting our heads around the terrain we'd soon be travelling through.

I had been to New York before on holiday but there was something about walking those streets that felt different this time. John and I were not there as tourists. We had brought something we had built and the city felt more welcoming somehow. Perhaps I imagined it, but it was as though we had earned our right to be there. I like to think it recognised something we hadn't had in us before.

We had lots of interesting meetings with friends and co-conspirators but one session stood out. Seeing Yancey Strickler, the co-founder and then CEO of Kickstarter. I'd been a little nervous to meet him. He was very gracious and said he'd always been a fan of our company and visited the site every month to keep an eye on our progress. He explained what they had set out to do. That their intention was to see whether it was possible to build what he called 'a medium-sized' internet company because they hated the monopolistic nature of web businesses that had emerged up until then.

We had an expansive chat about many things but the challenge he posed us was an incredibly simple, and personal, one. After he'd asked repeatedly how he could help, John and I looked at each other, seizing the moment, you could say, and opened up in a way I'm not sure either of us had planned to. We were very frank about our journey and how we were feeling – to each other as much as to him. I think it was because of what Kickstarter, Yancey and his co-founders Perry Chen and Charles Adler had come to represent in our heads. They had genuinely built a different kind of company. Even in the tech world, which revelled in its supposed radical newness. They and their brand had genuine authenticity. Kickstarter was the cross between a lighthouse and a place of pilgrimage for people like us. A business founded on principles we could relate to, but that was a huge financial success by anyone's standards. They might not be the only crowd-funding platform, but they were the one everyone else took their steer from. Alone among the start-up household names – the Amazons, Googles and Facebooks of this world – they actually stood for something other than the standard monopolistic bureaucracy that emerges alongside all new technologies.

Yancey suggested we were at a crucial moment in our journey. We were on the verge of something but it could still go wrong.

We had to be incredibly careful not to lose our way. Then, as a crucial component of what would help us find our path, he asked if we were sure we knew what 'success' meant. For us as founders. Were we sure we were aiming for what we considered to be success or someone else's definition of it?

He explained their 'stake in the ground' at Kickstarter was ensuring artists could fund their work without selling it. That was what drove all their decisions. It was their compass. He called it the 'rail we can always hold on to whatever we do'. They could always see where they were in relation to that purpose. He asked what ours was. We knew ours too. Books are the most successful mechanism for spreading ideas in human history. The way books come to be made matters. The people who choose what deserves to get published should be authors and readers themselves. That's what we set out to achieve. Creating a plat-form that gave all voices the chance to be heard. What 'success' meant personally, on the other hand, completely baffled me.

I admitted to him then that I have developed many faces on my journey running our company. I believe they are all consistent with who I am, but there is no doubt I show different aspects of myself, the different sides of my personality perhaps, depend-ing on who I'm talking to and when. Yancey challenged me on this fiercely, suggesting that at worst this could be dishonest, but even if not, it was potentially very damaging to me personally.

I bristled as he said it, but only because deep down I knew something in it was true. I didn't think I was doing anything dishonest, though. I'm just a contradictory, almost paradoxical, person like everyone else I've ever met. I change my mind about all kinds of things depending on when and where someone asks me. There is definitely part of me that wants and expects to build a globally disruptive company. And there's another side of me that wants to learn to surf and build chairs in the woods. But both 'faces' are 100 per cent me. Perhaps the trick was finding a way to inhabit both parts of myself within the structure and ethos of the company.

Yancey sent us off on our way with a suggestion that we put together a manifesto everyone associated with the business – investors, founders, employees and customers – could all read and sign up to. That's what he had just done. It had worked for them. Some people wouldn't like it, he said, but 'you can't please everyone'.

John and I emerged from his building and walked around Brooklyn pondering this simple but – at that moment – suddenly mesmerisingly profound question. What did success mean?

We talked about how far we'd come. Launching at Hay-on-Wye Festival in Wales six years before seemed a long way away and a long time ago. Justin, our other co-founder, was not with us and we missed him that afternoon. Family issues meant he'd been apart from us for a while. He was still active on the board and in the DNA of the company's vision but wasn't in the office day-to-day any more. Of course, for all of us at the start 'success' meant simply not going bust or losing control. Then 'success' became raising money. This is a potential landmine for many start-ups. So much of the language and conversation around tech companies comes from the people with the money. They have made entrepreneurs think that what they have – the money – is the rare commodity, but they are smart enough to know the truth. What's rare are great ideas and entrepreneurial teams who are either already brilliant or have the potential to be.

As long as our growth ambitions determined our trajectory, we would need to raise more money, so this was a world we would inhabit for a while longer. But we had to recognise we were faced with a different kind of challenge now as well. A company can always go bankrupt of course, but I mean we had to raise our sights from that 'drop dead' tension. Perhaps 'fear of failure' had allowed us to take our eyes off the real prize. We had to go for it. But for what, exactly?

John and I had a few pints and talked it through. We were both tired and very open about that even amidst all the excitement of what we had achieved and what we still wanted to do. We were in our seventh year of the business now. The company had been around for six but we'd spent a year before that trying to get it all off the ground. We'd been through a lot as friends and founders. And as a team.

My life had changed dramatically since we'd formed the company. After getting divorced in the early days of the business, I had got married the previous summer and my new wife and I had a baby son, Ted, who was born just before my seven-month fundraising process had begun. The juxtaposition of Ted's precious start in life with potentially the end of the company's, and mine and all my children's livelihood if I failed to raise that money, had put me under more pressure than I had ever felt in my life. It led to long stretches of thinking about the relationship between business and money what I was doing and how I could alleviate the tension. Driving back to Cornwall a few days earlier had made me realise just how much pressure I had been under when I'd come down to build the surfboard the year before. Now it was done. But I knew I was still readjusting.

When I arrived at the workshop to pick up the board so much had happened in the interim I didn't know what to say. I felt a sense of shame for having taken so long to collect it but also a surprising sense of closure that I had waited for the fundraise to be complete too. So I just hoped James understood. I had thought of the board often, using it as proof in my lowest moments that I was capable of delivering what was required of me. And building it had changed me. There had been signs since finishing it that I was evolving in small but powerful ways. It had certainly given me a new sense of confidence in myself that remained. I had a feeling that what I discovered about myself while building the board would continue to grow inside me.

He just smiled and nodded, asking if I was OK before drawing me into the kind of hug men give each other to concertina the time that has elapsed since they were last in the same place. I imagined how many other boards he had made since I last saw him as we let each other go. How many people had arrived following a path or arriving with inner questions of their own. You could just order a board from him online but he would always get you on the phone and try to persuade you to come and make it yourself. He was that kind of guy. Building a board was the bait that got you into his workshop, but by the time you left you realised what he really sold. The workshop had changed, though. It had an upstairs floor now. His wife Liz had joined the team. Otter Surfboards was evolving too.

He carried the board I'd made – a seven-foot-two 'Coaster' of his own design – out of the workshop and I was almost too scared to look at it. To see what I had made. He twisted the front of it towards me. Then I started to remember so much I had forgotten about that week. The planing. The gluing. The sanding. And what was written inside. My lips trembled at the thought of those words. He smiled at me and I took the board from him. It was lighter than I remembered. I ran my hands along the edges. I saw in the shape of it a reflection of what building it had enabled me to become. I'll admit that I did tear up a little then.

Because he was right. I could build something with *Spielzeug*. I couldn't deny it then.

We went down to the beach of the world I had stared at a year ago that night in June. The tide was out, so walking between the cliffs and seeing the horizon expand ahead into a seemingly endless succession of waves added to the poignancy. I rested the bottom of the board on the sand and stared, holding it in front of my body, pointing it towards the waves. I looked back to my left towards the cliff that hid the grassy bank I had run up from the other beach on the fourth day. I closed my eyes and ran my fingers along it as I had done in his workshop to tell whether it was 'done'. I had berated myself for not collecting it sooner but, strangely, now I was there, with the wind in my face, standing on that beach for the first time, it felt like the right moment had finally come.

I had built it. I had changed the perception of who I could become. I felt a renewed sense of energy about the way the business was evolving and what could be done.

I would continue to let go of the restrictive definition of myself I had carried in my life for so long. I just had to keep going. Doing what I felt had meaning. Continuing along the autotelic's path. Finding *Spielzeug* in people, ideas, places and things. If I did that, the obstacles I had spent my life putting in my own way would gradually be overcome. I accepted there would be no sanctuary from the anxiety of life if I had the courage to live before I died. Standing there with the sound of the water in my ears, I felt the anxious feeling in my stomach and realised anxiety and excitement were essentially the same thing. I was growing. Sometimes life made me anxious. Sometimes life made me excited. But it was never dull. I was curious about how mine might evolve in the years to come.

'Are you ready?' he said.

I nodded. Olive ran over from the car laughing and shouting, 'You can't surf, Daddy!' I leaned down, squeezed her and said I was going to learn and kissed her on the top of her head. She cartwheeled off across the sand. My twelve-year-old son Wilf, looking more like a surfer than I ever would with his long hair, came behind her wearing headphones and looked amazed. He took them off slowly. 'Did you really make that? Honestly?' I realised then I had changed the perception my eldest son had of me too. He looked at James, who nodded his assurance. Isobel appeared a few minutes later, holding little Ted in her arms. She handed him to me and took the board in her hands admiringly. 'It's beautiful,' she said, looking over at me smiling, not sounding or looking remotely surprised, before sitting down, resting it on her knees and running her fingers over it again and again.

I looked at what she had made in my arms while I was building the board the year before and buried my face in his neck, and tickled his shoulder blades, which made him giggle, a relatively new thing at the time. His brother and sister rushed over and did the same. I hugged and kissed the three of them in turn.

I thought about success then. It was the reflection of myself in their eyes that gave me the perspective to see it.

For me to feel success I have to find a balance between my internal self-belief and external validation. The perennial juxta-position between the internal journey and the external one.

I had to come to terms with my own narrative and personality and question my perception of who I could become. I had to challenge the pictures from my life I repeatedly focused on to question whether they really *had* to be the defining ones. But searching within myself alone would not be enough. It could lead to self-obsession. I had to 'be' out in the world too and do something to make my mark that others agreed had value. I had to connect, to put *Spielzeug* into something other people could feel. Whether it was through my writing, my relationships, by building a surfboard or the company I run. I had to have the courage to live with love, to be vulnerable and put myself out into the world, because that's where the *Spielzeug* we're all looking for comes from. The autotelic's path. If you would do what you're doing for its own sake, you are on the right one.

I thought about the lobster and the concept of growing through discomfort. 'Growth' was a big part of the corporate world lexicon. But I had my own definition I was now working on. I had grown through running the company because I had had to challenge my own presumptions about who I was and what I could do. I had realised at some point over the previous six months that whatever happened with the business, whatever 'exit' I might or might not get in financial terms, there was one thing I could rely on. There was an outcome I had already 'banked', so to speak. I had already achieved over 100 per cent growth in terms of my own story and this made me feel bulletproof as an entrepreneur whatever might happen with the company. It seemed to have opened the door to a different kind of motivation and ambition too.

When we started the business I saw no difference between me being successful and it being successful. I felt huge personal pressure that if the company failed it would mean I had failed. This fear is a colossal weight, but you must carry it if the business has not yet caught up with the vision you used at the start to motivate everyone. But if personal growth was my goal, then I had disconnected my sense of personal self-worth from the external success of the business, which might not actually have ever been entirely in my control anyway. This is the nub of the 'superman' CEO myth by the way. That it's all down to you. It's not. You are a part of the collective whole.

There are interesting implications for this if a business is successful too. In the scenario that your business is successful and you equate it with being synonymous with yourself, you will take personal credit for it, even if you did not grow and evolve as a person through the experience. If success happens too quickly, for example. So you will end up with the trappings, praise, status, money and inflated ego that come with success but not the self-value achieved through personal growth.That must feel very strange and perhaps account for why people who have 'got out' often feel unfulfilled and confused.

The more I thought about it, the corporate world seemed to be stuck in a kind of creationist thinking when it came to leadership. Blind to the way it had the potential to evolve. Where were the business leaders who were listened to and admired in society because they are thought of as wise as well as 'strong'? I felt a new breed of entrepreneur was required. One interested in other dimensions of business alongside financial and personal power-related ones.

In the early days of Unbound I had reread Gandhi's autobiography, *The Story of My Experiments with Truth*, to try to get a steer on what I was about to embark on. It might sound a bit counterintuitive but I saw it as the perfect 'disruption' manual. After all, Gandhi managed to disrupt the British Empire at the height of its powers and start India on the path of independence. At the time the British Empire was arguably more powerful than Google, Facebook and the US Army today combined. Gandhi's ambition to end the colonialist rule was insanely ambitious. Yet he achieved it while maintaining humility. Perhaps even because of it. Through it. Nelson Mandela achieved something equally astonishing. Walking free from his prison on Robben Island to become the president of the new South Africa. Again, the scale of that ambition was almost ridiculous at the time he set out to oppose apartheid rule, yet he managed it and went on to govern with a sense of humility that inspired the world. Combining ambition and humility was my new preoccupation, because it seemed to give you potential to achieve things that financial incentives or the desire for personal power simply could not contend with. While the kinds of destiny they both achieved were well beyond me, the principle felt meaningful and worth exploring. So this was the path I decided I now wanted to try to walk, both inside and outside of myself.

Back on the beach Isobel took Ted, and James handed me the board with a beaming smile on his face. 'Come on then, brother.'

I had to cajole everyone into their wetsuits but as soon as they were ready Wilf and Olive charged towards the sea, laughing hysterically, only to stop when their feet reached the foaming water. We caught up with them and I urged everyone on.

Behind me Ted started laughing in Isobel's arms – his little legs wriggling uncontrollably – in anticipation of what was to come.

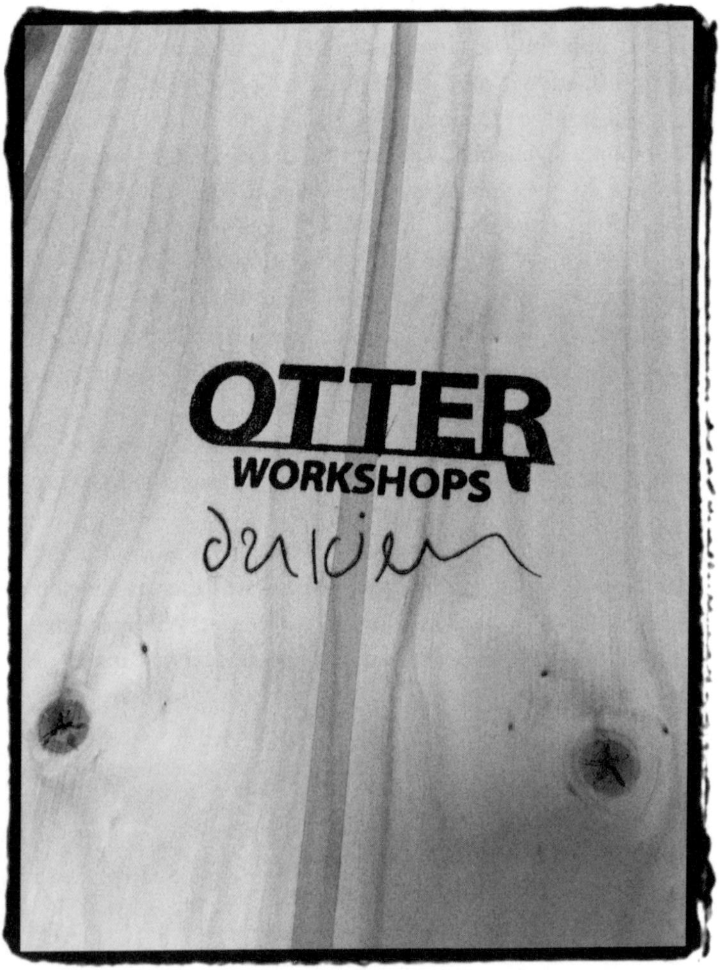
OTTER
WORKSHOPS

EPILOGUE

James told me the only way I could ever hope to actually stand and surf on the board I made would be by learning on another one first. 'This is much too good for you,' he said as he helped me strap it to the roof rack on my car later that afternoon. Four months on, I still haven't used it properly. Or arranged my first surfing lesson.

So the board is now leaning up against a bookcase in the office that, incidentally, contains most of the books Unbound has published so far. I see it every morning when I arrive at work. It reminds me who I am, and have the potential to become.

Sometimes when I lie in bed and drift off, in between wakefulness and sleep, the thought of the board emerges inside me. I can feel its presence where it is. It is quite happy for now. Content to bide its time. Knowing it has far more patience than me.

ABOUT THE AUTHOR

DAN KIERAN, described as a 'true disruptor' by Richard Branson, is the co-founder and CEO of Unbound.com, the award-winning crowdfunding publishing platform that brings authors and readers together, and the publisher of this book.

He is the author of twelve books, including the *Sunday Times* bestseller *Crap Towns* (the first viral internet phenomenon to turn into a bestselling book), *The Idle Traveller* (the bestselling *Slow Travel: Die Kunst des Reisens* in Germany) and *Three Men in a Float* (the story of his journey across England in a 1957 electric milk float). A travel writer for the *Guardian*, *The Times*, the *Telegraph* and *Die Zeit*, he also gives talks and workshops on raising money, entrepreneurship and how to have ideas.

ACKNOWLEDGEMENTS

A note on the text: I recorded an interview about *Spielzeug* with James in his workshop a few months before I went down to build the board, and I kept a detailed diary of the week I spent with him making it. This book draws on both, along with the slightly strained state of mind I spent the next twelve months drifting in and out of while I tried to raise our next round of investment.

Speaking to James's wife, Liz, it's clear I'm not alone in going to see him to build a surfboard only to find I've unlocked something in my mind by the end of the week. She says he is always exhausted when his workshops come to an end because he commits to them so completely. He's a truly remarkable man.

What I didn't realise in the week I built the board, or the year afterwards when I wrote this book in between meetings and childcare, is that by publishing it through Unbound I would gain a perspective on the company I could not have experienced in any other way. So the board didn't just unlock me. The business has evolved as a result too. The journey continues.

As well as thanking everyone at Unbound (all fifty of them and particularly DeAndra Lupu, my editor) and our many wise, excellent and good-looking investors (particularly Kerry

Baldwin, David Cummings, Sir David Verey, Dominic Perks, Nic Brisbourne, Paul Forster and our Chairman Christoph Sander), I also need to thank the people whose names appear in my list of subscribers. You did a wonderful thing. I have pledged for many books on Unbound, but only now do I realise how incredible it is as an author when someone pledges for your book. It's a vote of confidence delivered through an act of kindness, and every time anyone supported me I felt a life-affirming glow. It gives the company a kind of karmic, optimistic quality I'm proud to have discovered for myself.

In terms of the book, I need to thank John Lloyd for the story about the estate agent that he told me immediately after I told him about the idea of *Spielzeug* many years ago. It's still one of the most compelling examples of it I have ever come across. And to Roman Krznaric, Hilary Gallo, David Hieatt and Alex Smith for their generous feedback on the first draft.

I'm very lucky to have started a business with two generous, talented and wise men: John Mitchinson and Justin Pollard. They have both supported and helped me with this book and in my life in all kinds of ways over the last eight years. I love and respect them both very much.

I have written thirteen books over the last thirteen years, including this one, and I realised recently the three I'm proudest of have one thing in common. I wrote *I Fought the Law* on the kitchen table while my son Wilf was a toddler, *The Idle Traveller* while perched in my granny's armchair when my daughter Olive was starting to walk around, and this one on another kitchen table while my son Ted was crawling, and now walking, around too.

ACKNOWLEDGEMENTS

As a writer you always imagine one day having the perfect physical place to write in. One that is peaceful and quiet enough for the muse to take you. Perhaps a calm room overlooking a garden, with a roaring fire and a chaise longue under the window. But I've come to understand this is complete nonsense. The best books are the ones you write despite the distractions of a full-time job, small children and the chaos of your normal life going on around you. Because of them even. You have to really want to write them, for one thing. I think it's more than that though. Being a new parent does something to you. My children make me want to be the best version of me I can be. I think this is why I have succeeded in my own mind with these three books. In each I was trying to show each of them, and myself, what I'm made of. And despite failing in myriad ways, that fundamentally I'm made of good things.

Finally, I want to thank my wife, Isobel. This is for you, lovely one.

Unbound is the world's first crowdfunding publisher, established in 2011.

We believe that wonderful things can happen when you clear a path for people who share a passion. That's why we've built a platform that brings together readers and authors to crowdfund books they believe in — and give fresh ideas that don't fit the traditional mould the chance they deserve.

This book is in your hands because readers made it possible. Everyone who pledged their support is listed below. Join them by visiting unbound.com and supporting a book today.

Gunilla Andersson
Rob Ashelford
John Auckland
Morgan Bailey
Chris Barez-Brown
Christopher Beck
Tomas Begström
Jon Berry
Jack Birtwhistle
Mark Bottomley

Richard W Bray
Nic Brisbourne
James Brookes
Andrew Budden
Sorin Buga
Dan Burgess
Xander Cansell
Gianfranco Chicco
Mathew Clayton
David Cleevely

Julian Clyne

Mattias Collén

Philip Connor

James Cook

Harry Cooke

Nigel Cooke

Jason Cooper

Sarah Corbett

Chris Corbin

John Crawford

Helen Davies

Katie Davies

Martin Dehnberg

Steve Dimmick

Mary-Anne Driscoll

Paul Driver

Carole Edmond

Charles Fernyhough

James Fisher

Colin Forrest-Charde

Sarah Frankish

Dominic Frisby

Sören Gaardboe

Hilary Gallo

Tom Galloway

Andrea Gini

Charlie Gladstone

Charlie Gleason

Paul Goodison

Ele Gower

Katy Guest

Milo Herbert

Stuart Heritage

John Hesp

David Hieatt

E O Higgins

Chris Hines

Lars Hoff

Paul Holbrook

Niklas Järbur

Erik Jässi

Noelia Jimenez

Alice Jolly

Magnus Karlsson

Gareth Kieran

Isobel Kieran

Jill Kieran

Kevin Kieran

Olive Kieran

Ted Kieran

Wilf Kieran

Oliver Koch

Roman Krznaric

Andreas Laderer

Joris Lambert

Jimmy Leach

Stephen Leach

Luke Leighfield

Fiona Lensvelt

Tim LeRoy

Perttu Levijärvi

The Licudi

Henry Littlechild

Robert Loch

Richard Lonsdale

Elliott Mannis

John Mark

Julian Mash

Tim May

Graham McNicholl

Peter Meier

Carl Mesner Lyons

Andy Middleton

Jonny Miller

John Mitchinson

Virginia Moffatt

Kit Munday

Markus Naegele

Carlo Navato

Sarah Nelson

Nicklas Nilsson

Mats Nyström

OptiGroup AB

Justyna Pachniowska

Scott Pack

Michael Pagliari

Roland Palko

Lev Parikian

Kevin Parr

James Pembroke

Allan Persson

Stefan Petersson

Robert Phillips

Wouter Pijpers

Ben Pilgrim

Justin Pollard

David Roche

Ola Rosquist

Vilija Rugieniute

Anthea Salisbury

Christoph Sander

Stephan Serry

Stefan Sikander

Julian Simpson

Alex Smith

Chris Smith

Monika Somogyi

Truda Spruyt

Henrik Stadsing

Karsten Stadsing

Anna Stenstrand

Sönke Sudhoff

Kerry Symington

Jenö Szilagyi

James Taplin

Tot Taylor

Per Terp

Rowland Thomas

Jens Thuroe

Zdenko Topolovec

Michael Townsend

Ole Trommler

Bas van Es

Martin van Es

THE SURFBOARD

Alan Venables
Mark Vent
Sam Vines
Daniel Wallace
Jemima Webster
Volker Weinmann
Frank Weithase
Miranda West
Hannah Whelan
Andrew Wiggins
Suzie Wilde
Chris Wootton